FORTY HALL · ENFIELD

1629-1997

House, Courtyards, Walled Kitchen Garden
Pleasure Grounds, Park & Home Farm

by
Geoffrey Gillam

with a Foreword by
Brigadier Andrew Parker Bowles OBE

ENFIELD ARCHAEOLOGICAL SOCIETY

The Enfield Archaeological Society

Founded 1955

Membership of the Enfield Archaeological Society is open to all with an interest in the past.

The Society was formed in 1955 to recover, by means of the study and practice of archaeology, information about the history of the London Borough of Enfield. Sites investigated by the Society have included the pre-Roman earthwork at Bush Hill Park, the area of the Roman settlement at Bush Hill, as well as the nearby Roman Road known as Ermine Street, which ran through Edmonton and Enfield, the Tudor royal palaces at Elsyng, Forty Hall and at Enfield Town, the New River and many smaller domestic and industrial sites.

During the winter months there are illustrated lectures and in the summer there are occasional coach and other visits to places of interest.

Those who wish to take a more active part in the work of the Society are encouraged to carry out research into various aspects of the local history and archaeology of the London Borough of Enfield.

From time to time, as occasions demand, rescue excavations are carried out where archaeological sites are threatened.

Society News, a quarterly bulletin, which is free to members, gives details of forthcoming events, reports of past meetings, news of local archaeological discoveries and the results of research by members.

Previous publications include: *Prehistoric and Roman Enfield*, *The Royal Palaces of Enfield*, *The Industrial Monuments in the London Borough of Enfield*, *Enfield at War 1914-18*, *Enfield at War 1939-45*, *Histories and Mysteries of Writing and Theatres, Music Halls and Cinemas in the London Borough of Enfield*. Unfortunately, these are now out of print. Other publications are in the course of production.

The Society is affiliated to the Council for British Archaeology and the London and Middlesex Archaeological Society.

For details of membership, please contact:

The Enfield Archaeological Society,

23 Merton Road, Enfield, Middx EN2 0LS. Telephone 0181 367 0263.

© Enfield Archaeological Society 1997

ISBN 0 9501877 2 0

Published by the Enfield Archaeological Society
23 Merton Road Enfield Middlesex EN2 0LS

Designed and produced by Mayfield Books, Mayfield, Ashbourne, Derbys
Printed by The Cromwell Press Ltd, Boughton Gifford, Wilts

Contents

	Foreword	page 4
	Illustrations	5
	Preface	6
	Acknowledgements	7
1	Historical Introduction	9
2	The House — Exterior	15
3	The House — Interior	28

    Great Hall • 28
    Staircase Passage • 30
    South-East (Drawing) Room • 31
    Steward's Room, Buttery & Pantry • 31
    Middle Room • 33
    South-West (Rainton) Room • 34
    Servants' Hall • 35
    First Floor • 36
    Second Floor • 38
    Basement • 39
    Sanitation • 40
    Water Supplies • 40
    Heating & Lighting • 40
    Furniture • 40

4	The Courtyards	41

    Inner Courtyard • 41
    Kitchen • 42
    Outer Courtyard • 43

5	The Grounds	47

    Front Lawn & Lake • 47
    Pleasure Grounds • 49
    Walled Kitchen Garden • 52
    Rabbit Warren • 54
    The Park • 54

	Appendices	59

    Appendix One — Arms Displayed in First Floor Landing Windows • 59
    Appendix Two — The King Arthur Cross • 61
    Appendix Three — Arms Displayed on the Rainton Tomb • 62

	References	63

Foreword

I spent the first eleven years of my life at Forty Hall. It was my family's house. Because of my father's tuberculosis he was advised to move, so he sadly sold Forty in 1951. Living for just eleven years in a house with a history going back three hundred and sixty-five years would not normally give me the honour of writing a foreword to this learned and highly enjoyable book. However, there is no-one else alive who lived in Forty for as long as I did whilst it was still a family's home.

I have been back fairly often over the last twenty years to Enfield and to Forty Hall and Myddleton house in particular. The latter house bordered with Forty and belonged to E. A. Bowles, my great-great uncle and one of England's 'greatest amateur gardeners'.

On one of these visits I took the Duchess of Devonshire, who is renowned for her good taste, wisdom and knowledge of the Arts, to see Forty Hall. She gazed at the house from across the lake and said that in her opinion it was one of the most perfectly proportioned and beautiful houses in England.

Until I read Geoffrey Gillam's fascinating and deeply researched book, I thought I knew all there was to know about Forty and its grounds and farm. I had after all as a boy roamed the whole estate (children in those days could roam by themselves without the human danger present nowadays). I had followed Mr Miles the gamekeeper as he shot vermin in the woods. I had helped Mr Taylor the farm foreman tack up the shire horses who pulled the wagons filled with wheat sheaves to the stackyard. I had checked every pond, stream and water hole for newts and frog-spawn. I had climbed on and inspected roofs, cellars and dusty attics. This book goes into such detail that I now realise how little all of us knew about Forty and also how much dedicated work has gone into it.

Possibly the ideal place to read Geoffrey Gillam's *Forty Hall* would be on an early summer's afternoon sitting facing the house under the spreading branches of the Lebanese cedar, which I now have learnt is over three hundred years old.

I have nothing but admiration and gratitude for the author and this work he has produced.

I must also record my thanks to the Borough Council of Enfield for keeping Forty Hall and its grounds in such a wonderful state and allowing so many people to visit and enjoy it.

I am grateful also to the Enfield Archaeological Society for their interest and work in preserving Forty and in discovering new facts about its history.

If the outer farm courtyard and the ancient farm buildings could be restored and once put into use, Forty Hall would again be, as it used to appear to me as a schoolboy, heaven on earth.

Brigadier Andrew Parker Bowles OBE

Illustrations

	Forty Hall at night	*front cover*	28	Ceiling of north-east room on first floor	37
	Pen and ink drawing of Forty Hall 1884 *title page*		29	Ceiling of south-east room on first floor	37
1	Air photograph of Forty Hall and Grounds c1965 (Hunting Aerofilms A147305)	8	30	Drawing of chimney piece in middle room on first floor	39
2	Sir Nicholas Rainton 1643	9	31	Plaster mask on ceiling of south-east room on second floor	39
3	Rainton family monument	9	32	Gateway to inner courtyard	41
4	James Meyer II	13	33	Entrance to outer courtyard today	44
5	Sir Henry Ferryman Bowles	14	34	Entrance to outer courtyard c1900	44
6, 7	Plans attached to sale catalogue 1773	16	35	Stables in outer courtyard	45
8	Forty Hall Estate. (Reproduced from Ordnance Survey 25in plans 1936 Middx II)	17	36	Main barn in outer courtyard	45
9	Pen and Ink drawing of Forty Hall 1823	18	37	Building in south-west corner of outer courtyard	46
10	Forty Hill from The Goat public house, looking north	19	38	Excavations on north lawn 1993	47
11	Entrance gates to Forty Hall	19	39	17th century drain in north lawn	48
12	Lodge, side view	20	40	Brickwork across middle of north lawn	49
13	Lodge, front view	20	41	Garden mount, now covered with trees	50
14	Front view of house 1894	21	42	View from second floor window of house, north lawn, lake and avenue of trees	50
15	Rear of house 1894	22	43	Basil, the head gardener, standing at the north end of the kitchen garden, 1894	52
16	Front and east view of house 1932	23	44	Well-head in walled kitchen garden	53
17	Rear view of house c1980	24	45	Avenue of trees and house	56
18	View of house and lake from the north	24	46	View across lower lake	56
19	Plan of house 1636	26	47	Bridge abutments in Maidens Brook at the northern end of the avenue of trees	58
20	Plan of house 1951	27	48	Brick foundations on edge of lower lake after excavation 1992	58
21	Screen in Great Hall	29	49	Arms in landing windows	59
22	Fireplace in Great Hall	29	50	The King Arthur Cross	61
23	Main staircase	30	51	Arms displayed on the Rainton tomb	62
24	Fireplace in south-east (drawing) room	31		Arms in landing windows	*rear cover*
25	Ceiling of south-east (Drawing) room	32			
26	Present reception, formerly steward's room	32			
27	South-west (Rainton) room	34			

Preface

Forty Hall is one of a group of houses around London built during the first half of the 17th century by self-made City men who wanted a relatively small country house which incorporated the best features of grander residences elsewhere with the ideals of comfort and grandeur compressed into a compact plan. In the case of Forty Hall, the house was designed to meet the needs of one man — Nicholas Rainton — and, as one would expect, successive owners have each made changes to suit their own requirements and to incorporate the latest ideas and fashions as they were introduced. This has resulted in many alterations and additions to the house and associated buildings, as well as to the grounds, over a long period of time, making it difficult to disentangle its history. A previous writer expressed it well with her remarks that '... Forty Hall is thus a more complicated house than at first appears. It is not an easy house to understand ...' (HARWOOD).

Nevertheless, by reading the printed sources, examining surviving documents, looking at photographs, drawings and paintings, studying the cartographic evidence, speaking to people who knew the house when it was a private residence, and corresponding with others, many new facts have emerged. An examination of the house with its added and rebuilt staircases, blocked doorways, extensions and other structural alterations, as well as a detailed study of the gardens, pleasure grounds and park has also provided much new information and has resulted in a greater understanding of the history and development of the house and grounds.

Inventories, especially if they list the house owner's goods room by room are very helpful in establishing the original purpose of each room. Unfortunately, the situation did not arise which necessitated the preparation of such an inventory for Forty Hall. However, we do have two 18th century sale catalogues which give many details. The first attempted sale in 1773 was unsuccessful but the catalogue was retained and apart from minor alterations the same format was used for the later sale in 1787.

Local histories from Lysons onwards contain useful information. In the case of Lysons, as well as quoting references where the documents concerned are no longer available, he also indulges in flights of fancy where he feels the need to supply a missing answer. There is also the material collected by Richard Gough from 1771 until his death in 1809 for his proposed History of Enfield, the notes for which are now in the Bodleian Library. A note, in another hand, at the front of the volume of papers states that they were 'practically adopted wholesale without any acknowledgement' by William Robinson as the basis for his *History of Enfield* published in 1823. The note goes on to say that Gough's abbreviations led to many 'ludicrous mistakes' — made by later copyists. There are more, albeit meagre, details to be gleaned from the local newspapers. Volume five of the *Victoria County History* for Middlesex contains a summary of the history of Forty Hall, and there are, of course, the three volumes of David Pam's *History of Enfield* published between 1990 and 1994 which contain many more references. Printed guides have been prepared from time to time by the London Borough of Enfield since the house was opened as a museum, but the contents of some early editions have to be treated with caution.

A lot more has been discovered about the lives of the people who lived at Forty Hall although many details still remain obscure; what was the exact nature of the 'misconduct' of the sons of Eliab and Elizabeth Breton? And, what was the cause of the financial disaster that overtook Edmund Armstrong resulting in several cases being heard in the Court of Chancery? More research is necessary before full answers can be given to these and other questions.

Many years ago members of the Medieval Research Group of the Enfield Archaeological Society researching the history of Elsyng Palace came across several references to Forty Hall which proved useful when preparing this account. There are many photographs of Forty Hall from the 19th century to the present day in the Local History Library of the London Borough of Enfield, and there are others in the National Monuments record, all of which provided details of architectural changes that have taken place to the house.

Apart from the Ordnance Survey 25in plans published in 1865, 1896, 1913 and 1936, there are 18th century plans which are large enough in scale to give details of Forty Hall and its grounds. When the estate was put up for auction in 1773 it was divided into lots for each of which a separate and detailed plan was drawn. There is also a large scale plan showing the land holdings in Enfield of Eliab Breton at the time of his death in 1785. This plan is particularly interesting as it shows not only the outlines of some of the common fields of Enfield but also individual strips within each field. More plans were drawn for each of the lots comprised in the sale of 1787. Fourteen years later, the Enclosure Act of 1801 with its accompanying plan show the last remnants of the medieval agricultural system just before they were swept away. There is also Roque's map of Middlesex published in 1754, but although it is useful the scale is too small to provide the detailed information required for the study of Forty Hall and its grounds.

The gardeners who were responsible for the original layout and subsequent modification of the gardens, pleasure grounds and park at Forty Hall remain unrecognised. However, fieldwork and excavation have revealed some of the features they installed; terracing and by implication parterres, a belt walk, raised walks, sites of summerhouses, a garden mount, the avenue of lime trees and its associated water feature, as well as mini cascades in Maidens brook.

Acknowledgements

I am grateful to many people for their contributions; to John Griffin, Museums Officer, for providing access to all parts of Forty Hall, making available the collection of paintings and drawings of the house and the thesis dealing with 17th century plaster ceilings. To Graham Dalling, local History Librarian for the London Borough of Enfield, and his assistants Kate Godfrey and Maureen Austen for their help and hospitality during my visits to the library to look at the collection of printed sources, sale catalogues, newspaper files, photographs and documents housed there. To Charles Kingdom who was able to tell me much about Forty Hall and the staff needed to run the house between c1924 and the Second World War. To Mrs M. Newton for drawing my attention to the article in *Country Life*, which included references to Forty Hall. To Dave Howlett, senior caretaker at Forty Hall who has long had a keen interest in the building and its history. Over the years he has noted a great deal of information received from people who had known the house when it was a private residence. To Ted Bonham, also a caretaker at Forty Hall museum, for his help in opening otherwise closed rooms during my visits. To Dr A. McGuire for providing information regarding research by Professor A Gomme and herself on smaller country houses. To Mike Cole who farmed at Forty Hall for permission to explore the 'lane from Forty Hall to the New River', 'the walks and double hedges', and the sites of former summer houses. To John Sykes who identified the artist responsible for the painting of Forty Hall in 1793 and his comments regarding the scene portrayed as a fete champetre. Unfortunately, he was unable to locate the present owner of the painting. The photograph appearing in *Country Life* was later reproduced in WORSLEY and I am grateful to John for drawing my attention to this latter publication, which also contains other references to Forty Hall. John made visits to the Public Record Office, the Bodleian Library and the Guildhall Library to obtain more information about the previous owners of Forty Hall and to Norton where he discovered the funeral hatchment of Eliab Breton in the church; disappointingly, the Breton family house had been demolished in 1951. To Ian Jones, who provided the suggested alignment for the staircase prior to the alterations of 1897. To Andrew Cooke, Conservation Manager, and Christine White, of the Department of Planning and Building Control of the London Borough of Enfield, for making available details of Forty Hall from their files. To Irene Smith, Secretary of Enfield Preservation Society, for kindly supplying copies of correspondence dated 1929 which give details of properties in Enfield held by the late Mrs Parker Bowles. To John McDonagh, Senior Surveyor of the London Borough of Enfield, for providing plans of Forty Hall which helped enormously with my attempts to record original features and to work out the sequence of later alterations. To Robert Whytehead of English Heritage for keeping me informed about test pits dug in the outer courtyard and barn and to Derek Seeley of the Museum of London Archaeology Service for providing me with copies of the reports of the findings made during the digging of the pits. To Andrew Wittrick, an historian with English Heritage, for providing me with a copy of his report on the stable block, the main barn and the garden house in the outer courtyard, on which I have drawn freely. His helpful comments about features of 17th century houses and in particular his remarks regarding the likelihood of a privy being located in the recess next to the chimney breast in the Rainton Room, led me to look more closely at this part of Forty Hall. To the staff of the National Monuments Record, Royal Commission of Historical Monuments Office in London, the Libraries department of the London Borough of Enfield and Hunting Aero Surveys for permission to use photographs from their collections. To I.F. Wright, Archivist for HM Customs and Excise Library Services for information regarding the 4½% customs duties for Barbados 1663-1838. To Dr Linda Washington, Head of the Department of Printed Books, in the National Army Museum, for information regarding 18th century army agents and details of the lineage of regiments for whom Edmund Armstrong was the agent. To Pamela Clarke, Deputy Registrar of the Royal Archives, The Royal Collection Trust, Windsor Castle, for providing details of Edmund Armstrong's appointments within the Lord Chamberlain's Department. To Bernard Nurse and his colleague at the Library of the Society of Antiquaries for help in tracing the dates on which Edmund Armstrong and subsequently his son were elected as fellows. To David Pam who generously provided me with copies of his notes regarding Edwyn Rich and the Dower House and of Sir Hugh Fortey, which he had made when researching his *History of Enfield*. To Roger Eddington who, when visiting the exhibition of 'The Artist and the Country House, from the 15th century to the present day' at Sotheby's in 1995/6, spotted the painting by John Wooton (c1682-1765), *A View of London from the Terrace of Caenwood* (now Kenwood) House, Hampstead, which includes a scaled down version of a galleon on a lake in a similar situation to the one in Edward Daye's painting of Forty Hall. To Jon Tanner who prepared the plans of Forty Hall from the rough drafts submitted to him. To Patrick Streeter of Matching Green in Essex who kindly supplied me with copies of wills and a detailed family tree of the Meyer family. To Richard Coxshall who drew my attention to the photograph of Forty Hill, taken in the early years of the 20th century, and which was subsequently donated by Phillip Armitage to the Local History Library. To the Ordnance Survey Office for permission to reproduce the 25in plans showing Forty Hall and its grounds. To Barbara Smith for help with typing the draft of the publication. In particular to Peter Gillam who completed the initial draft and for making subsequent amendments to prepare the text for publication. Finally, to Ian Jones, John Sykes and John Stevens who read the draft and offered helpful comments and criticisms.

However, I alone am responsible for opinions and interpretations expressed in this publication.

Geoffrey Gillam

1 Air photograph of Forty Hall and grounds c1965. Part of the excavated remains of Elsyng Palace can be seen to the right of the avenue of trees. (Hunting Aerofilms, A147305)

1
Historical Introduction

Nicholas Rainton, 1569-1646, a rich London merchant, having purchased the manor of Worcesters in 1616 from Sir Robert Cecil, Earl of Salisbury (W1616), was to wait another thirteen years before building Forty Hall on part of his manorial lands. However, the fact that he rented a pew in St Andrews church from 1620 at least (P1620) for use during his extended visits means that he would have needed a place of residence in Enfield before his new house was ready in 1632-3. A candidate was one of two houses standing not far from the site of the later Forty Hall. Nicholas Rainton owned property in Forty Hill, later to become known as the Dower House, which may have formed part of his original purchase of the manor of Worcesters. At first glance, the architectural evidence suggests that the present building is of early-mid 17th century date — a mural over a fireplace is said to have been dated to 1640 (HERITAGE) — and therefore roughly contemporary with Forty Hall, but the record of a dispute in the 18th century regarding the amount of rent to be paid implies that what appears to be the Dower House, described in the document concerned, is a much earlier building. In 1770, the lessees of this house claimed that in view of extensive repair work carried out in the 1630s by Edwyn Rich, the lessee at the time, he was given a new lease and a reduced rent by Nicholas Rainton in 1637, which suggests that the present Dower House may be a lot earlier in origin than hitherto believed. At the same time Edwyn Rich was given permission to

2 Sir Nicholas Rainton 1643

3 (right) The Rainton tomb in Enfield Parish Church

demolish another, even older, house imperfectly located to the west (PROa). It is possible therefore that Nicholas Rainton lived either in the Dower House or in the nearby older house during his visits to Enfield from c1616 until his new residence was constructed next door — which would have been a suitable location from which to monitor the progress of building work. Access between the two properties certainly existed as shown by the blocked gateway in the south wall of the kitchen garden at Forty Hall. This gateway does not appear to have been open for very long as it is filled with 17th century brickwork identical in type and laid in a similar, irregular, bond as the rest of the wall.

Nicholas Rainton also purchased the remainder of the lease of Enfield Palace in the centre of Enfield Town in 1630 (LYSONSa) but there is no evidence to suggest that he ever stayed there. He remained an active business man in the City long after his house was built in Enfield — we know that he moved his premises in Lombard Street to Cornhill in April, 1634 (TAYLOR) and he did not finally retire to Forty Hall until 1642; his coach emblazoned with his arms, his coachmen, armed outriders and pages in attendance, dressed in his livery, would have been a familiar sight as it passed through Enfield Town on its way to and from the City of London. He made his money by importing satin and taffeta from Florence and velvet from Genoa — being a staunch puritan he no doubt came to terms with his conscience regarding this trade. A leading member of the Haberdashers' Company, he became an Alderman of the City of London, Aldgate ward, in 1621, Sheriff in 1621-22 and was elected Lord Mayor in 1632, being knighted in the following year. There is a portrait of him in St Bartholomew's Hospital, of which he was President from 1634 until his death, and another can be seen in Forty Hall.

He not only refused to lend money to Charles I but he also failed to supply details of the wealth of his associates when requested to do so by the Crown, for which he was briefly imprisoned in 1640. Taken to the Marshalsea, he was then moved to the Tower with four other aldermen but, following public demonstrations, they were all released after only five days imprisonment. His sympathies with Parliament waned after the outbreak of the Civil War in 1642 when in that year he turned down the offer of a place on the Committee of Safety on the grounds of 'many other employments' and retired to Forty Hall (PEARL); age and infirmity, as well as prudence, may have prompted this decision.

Sir Nicholas Rainton died at Forty Hall in 1646. By this time his son and daughter-in-law and all six grandchildren were dead, together with his wife Rebecca, nee Moulton, who he had married at St Christopher le Stock church in London in November 1602, who had pre-deceased him six years earlier, and their elaborate family monument, restored a few years ago, can be seen in St Andrew's Church where they are buried in one of three vaults below the vestry room. The monument consists of a three-tiered structure with, at the top, a reclining figure of Sir Nicholas clad in armour and wearing the robes, collar and badge of a Lord Mayor of London. Below is an effigy of his wife, Lady Rebecca, reading the ten commandments and, at the bottom the figures of his son (also Nicholas) his daughter in law (also Rebecca) and those of their sons and daughters in two groups behind their parents. On the pediment of the monument are the arms of Rainton with those of Wolstenholme above. On either side are smaller shields; that on the left carries the arms of Rainton and Moulton, and those on the right the arms of Moulton only. The estate was inherited by the great nephew of Sir Nicholas, who was also Nicholas and at that time still a minor (LYSONS b).

North of Forty Hall stood all that remained of Elsyng Palace (PALACES) which in 1641 had been purchased from the Crown by Phillip Herbert, Earl of Pembroke, who appears to have lived there until his death in 1650 (CALENDAR a). By 1656 the palace buildings were in the possession of Nicholas Rainton (R1656) and they were demolished soon afterwards, the ground was levelled and the site became part of the park attached to Forty Hall.

In 1683 Nicholas was suspected of concealing conspirators involved in the Rye House plot, who had planned to kill Charles II and his brother James during their journey from Newmarket to London but, although Forty Hall was searched by soldiers, no evidence was found to connect Nicholas with the plotters and no further action was taken against him (CALENDAR b). Like his great-uncle before him, Nicholas continued to enclose common land in Enfield in the face of considerable local opposition, battling in the courts and often, literally, in the fields concerned over this issue (PAM a). His daughter Mary married Sir John Wolstenholme, who lived at Minchenden, in Enfield church in 1675 and on the death of Nicholas in 1696 the estate came into the couple's possession. In 1698 it was settled on their son — yet another Nicholas; later Sir Nicholas Wolstenholme — after his marriage to Grace the daughter of Sir Edmund Waldoe. By 1707 he was so much in debt that the estate was put into the hands of trustees who continued to administer it, with many economies being made, until his death in 1716. In 1717/18 his widow married William Ferdinand Carey, Lord Hunsdon, who was of Dutch extraction and he is recorded as improving the estate from its previously impoverished condition. Grace died in 1729 and as Lord Hunsdon had only been a 'tenant for (his wife's) life' Forty Hall passed to Elizabeth and Mary, nieces and co-heirs of Sir Nicholas Wolstenholme. Grace was buried at Hutton Rudbury in Yorkshire and Lord Hunsdon returned to the family seat in Holland where he died in 1765 aged 82. In 1740 Elizabeth married Eliab Breton. Mary who retained her part interest as co-heiress continued to live at Forty Hall until her death in 1763 (GOUGH).

The price of land rose sharply in the 18th century and Eliab Breton began selling some of his land and property in 1771 but much of it failed to reach the very high reserve prices he had set. Two years later Forty Hall and its grounds were offered for sale by auction but they too failed to reach their reserve (S P 1773).

A letter written by Richard Gough, who was Breton's neighbour, on 27th October, 1773 after his return from an excursion into Dorset especially for the sale, contains some pithy comment;

> ... to assist at the sale of Mr. Breton's estate which after having been pushed by Mr. Christie near half a year was put up under the hammer in his own house in 30 parcels divided by a farm and pieces contiguous to it and in the occupation of different persons, and to some of them absolutely necessary as our little piece of 3/4 acre to us. Mr. Christie had bargained for £1200 for the trouble in surveying and cataloguing the whole, and there was actually achieved no more than £3,000 worth sold at what was estimated at between £70 and £80,000 .... After disappointment in the value of his estate and house he [ie Breton] must remain in quiet possession with no more advantage than that of paying an advanced land tax according to the rents he has publicly owned in print ....' (GOUGH).

It is not clear why Eliab Breton had wanted to sell Forty Hall. He does not appear to have had any financial problems at the time but as the family seat was at Norton in Northamptonshire, where he retained land holdings, it may have been his wish to return there. He certainly visited Norton and his wife Elizabeth gave birth to Mary, their first child there in 1742. Although a few other parcels of land were sold, no other attempt was made to sell Forty Hall and he and his wife continued to live there for another twelve years. Eliab Breton died in 1785 and his body was interred in the family vault at Norton. There had been several children but only three sons, Michael Harvey, William and Eliab, survived him. His married daughter Mary, who had three sons, died in 1767. Three other children died in infancy (GOUGH & GENTS MAG b). In a long and detailed will, drawn up in 1778, which ran to eleven pages, including two codicils added in 1785, he left the bulk of his estate to his wife Elizabeth with instructions concerning bequests to his three sons and three grandsons. Land in Kent was to be sold to provide annuities of £400 for each of his two youngest sons, William and Eliab. Michael Harvey his eldest son, was to receive £1,000, William Cooke the sum of £100 and each of the cottage tenants at Norton a lump sum or a year free of rent. His grandsons, Charles, John and William Hope, the children of his deceased daughter Mary, were to receive the interest on an invested sum of £1,000 for each of them. The first codicil to the will increased the amount held in trust for each of his grandsons to £2,000. The second codicil gave his servant Henry Turnbull an annuity of £10 to be paid half yearly (PRO b)

However, things did not go according to plan and in 1787 his widow was forced to sell Forty Hall and all the remaining land holdings in Enfield which were 'dismembered under Mr. Christie's hammer, through the misconduct of their offspring' (GENTS MAG a). The nature of this misconduct is not known; it could have been the result of unwise speculation or even gambling debts. In any event, after the debts had been settled Mrs. Breton moved to a house in Pall Mall where she died in 1790. Her obituary describes how well she bore up under the strain of seeing 'her paternal fortune dissipated. A lesson to those immediately related to her'. She left the lease of her house, the furniture and her belongings to her three grandsons — her income, no doubt derived from a small annuity, ceased with her death. There was no mention of her sons in her will (PRO c). William married and had two daughters but the fate of Eliab is not known. Michael Harvey is referred to in the family tree as 'of Norton and of Enfield' (BAKER) so it is therefore likely that he continued to occupy Forty Hall after his father's death in 1785 until forced to sell to redeem outstanding debts. He had married and there was a son and a daughter, neither of whom were to inherit the manor of Norton. There were further financial problems and in 1794 the Norton estate was vested in trustees and it must have been at this time that he moved to Epping Green near Little Berkhampstead, where he died in 1798. It took the trustees another two years to sort out his affairs and to arrange the sale of the manor of Norton, the proceeds from which must have been used to settle the further debts he had incurred (GOUGH).

The 1787 sale catalogue is almost identical to the one prepared for the abortive sale fourteen years earlier (SP 1787). Lot one consisted of:

Forty Hall, and the lands usually occupied therewith, together with the extensive manor of Worcester, and all Finds, Herriots, Reliefs, Quit Rents, Royalties, Suits, Services, and Emoluments thereafter belonging ...

			A	R	P
1	THE MANSION HOUSE, with the Yards, Courts, Outbuildings, Gardens, Ponds, Lawns, Walks, Plantations, &c, &c containing together		12	1	30
2	Great Field	Meadow	47	1	28
3	Pond Groves (pond included)	Ditto	14	0	10
4	Primrose Hill	New laid	9	3	14
5	Upper Primrose Hill (wooded)	Ditto	12	1	6
6	The Warren	Meadow	12	0	20
8	Long Field	Ditto	11	2	0
9	Rush Croft	Ditto	3	3	3
10	Eight Acres	Ditto	7	3	23
11	Willow Grove	Ditto	8	2	12
12	Lower Hutchings Meadow	Ditto	8	0	32
13	Upper Hutchings Meadow	Ditto	4	2	14
14	Little Hutchings	Ditto	1	0	30
15	A small orchard adjoining the New River (in which are 9 fruit trees)		0	1	8
	The lane from Forty Hall down to the New River		2	1	20
	The Walk and double hedges		2	0	16
76	A barn and small field at Forty Hall occupied by John Field, Tenant at Will		0	1	36
	Total		159	0	19

The 159 acres comprising Lot One were purchased for £8,800 at auction in May 1787 by Edmund Armstrong who at that time was living at Percy Street, Rathbone Place in London. He continued to maintain his London address which gave him a town house and with his newly acquired property in Enfield he now had a place in the country as lord of the manor of Worcesters. The Armstrongs were a well established family from the Anglo-Irish Ascendancy, with numerous military connections and the occasional high office of state. Edmund Armstrong's father was Comptroller of the Household to the Lord Lieutenant of Ireland and his brother Andrew lived at the family seat of Garry Castle in Kings County, now Offaly, not far distant from Dublin (BURKE).

A copy of the 1787 sale catalogue for Forty Hall is endorsed in Richard Gough's hand to the effect that the house and grounds had been sold '... to Captain Armstrong for £8,800'. No other document gives him a military rank and a glance at the army lists for the 18th century failed to locate him. In the notices confirming his various appointments and in his subsequent obituaries he is referred to as plain Edmund and Burke's Commoners of 1838 confirms the lack of military rank. From 1777 he was Husband of the 4½% Duties in the Customs, which was a grant made in 1663 by the legislature of Barbados to Charles II of 4½% in kind on the exportation of all dead goods grown or purchased in the island. The duties were repealed in 1838 (WRIGHT). He became a member of the Royal Household, within the Lord Chamberlain's department when he was appointed a Gentleman Usher Quarterly Waiter in 1779, a position he held until 1794, when he became one of the four grooms of the Privy Chamber to George III (CLARK). Both these posts, like the 4½% plantation duties, were well paid sinecures, the obtaining of which owed much to family connections. The French declared war on Britain in February 1793. Fearful of invasion and the spread of sedition from the French Revolution the Vestry formed a committee in December 1792 to defend the Constitution. Local gentlemen were invited to join and two years later, in June 1794, Edmund Armstrong was co-opted (VESTRY). It was in 1794 that he also became an army agent to the 3rd, 20th, 54th, 94th and 111th regiments of foot (GENTS MAG c) — an army agent was responsible for the disbursement of pay, clothing and accoutrements for serving officers and other ranks of the regiments concerned, for which he was paid a commission.

A few years earlier in 1789, Edmund had been elected a Fellow of the Society of Antiquaries (FSA); Fellowships were often sought in those days for the social cachet they gave rather than antiquarian interest on the part of the persons seeking nomination. It is interesting to note that Richard Gough, who was a neighbour of Armstrong, was also a Fellow of the Society of Antiquaries but his name does not appear on the list of the three proposers against Armstrong's name. He married twice. His first wife was a Miss Mackie, by whom he had a daughter 'who died young'. His second marriage was to Frances or Fanny Armstrong — a cousin — by whom he had two sons; William Archibald, born in 1770 and George Andrew, born in 1771 and a daughter Hariot Anne (BURKE). Edmund Armstrong died in 1797, aged 62. The notice in *The Times* newspaper reporting his death at his London home stated; 'No public panegyric need be added — the feelings of thousands of individuals will testify his virtues' (TIMES a). He left massive debts, as yet not fully explained. This financial catastrophe seems to have been foreseen by the family a few years earlier as what appears to have been an attempt to transfer the Forty Hall estate to William Archibald with a mortgage of £7,000 took place in 1792 (PRO d). Although Edmund had made a will it was drawn up in Percy Street in 1786, two years before he purchased Forty Hall (PRO e). Following his death, William Archibald was appointed as administrator of the estate and by paying the funeral expenses and settling some of the debts, with promises to pay the remainder, he did his best to keep the Forty Hall estate within the family. However, more debts became known and there were actions through the Court of Chancery by the parties concerned (CHANCERY). The largest claim was 'by the solicitor for His Majesty's Attorney General, who on behalf of His Majesty had claimed before him a debt of £21,667 4s 9½d against the estate of Edmund Armstrong ...' (PRO f). John Wilmot, a master of the Court of Chancery, was appointed to deal with the situation and ordered that details of the case be advertised so that any further claimants could come forward by a given date.

As a result of the claims made by John Armstrong (cousin) on behalf of himself and unsatisfied creditors v William Archibald (eldest son) and others; Francis (wife of Edmund), George (son) and Hariot Anne (daughter) (PRO f), an order was made for the sale of Forty Hall and the house in Percy Street. Forty Hall was put up for sale by auction on 7th November 1799 (SP 1799).

It is not known what happened to Frances Armstrong or to the daughter Hariot Anne; it is hoped members of the family came to the rescue. George Andrew pursued a career in the army and rose to the rank of Lieutenant-General. He married twice — his second wife was Mary Esther, daughter of T.A. Russell of Cheshunt Park. The eldest son — The Reverend William Archibald Armstrong BA FSA — in 1794, he too was elected a Fellow of the Society of Antiquaries — continued to live in Enfield, where in 1796 he had married Charlotte the younger daughter of Richard Hassell of Cheshunt Park (BURKE). For a period of two years he lived at the Rectory Manor in Parsonage Lane (ROBINSON a). As lecturer in Enfield church he received an annual grant from the Henry Loft Charity (ROBINSON b). By 1803 he had become a curate at Cheshunt church, a position he still held in 1817 (GENTS MAG d). He became a magistrate for the counties of Hertford and Middlesex; in 1814 he dealt with irregularities in the accounts of one of the Enfield benefit clubs, and in 1822 he clashed with the select vestry regarding the lack of care being given to a local family who were in considerable distress (PAM b). As rector of Hykeham in Lincolnshire he received the income from tithes — income would have been important to William Archibald as he had eleven children to support (BURKE).

James Meyer was the eventual purchaser of the Forty Hall estate for which he paid £11,940; he actually took possession on Lady Day 1800 (GOUGH). A wealthy London merchant of Dutch extraction, whose family name was originally Meijer, he was a member of the Dutch Reformed Church and several of the family monuments could be seen in the Dutch church at Austin Friars in London until they were destroyed during an air raid in 1940. Fortunately, details of the various monuments, including those of the Meyer family, were published in 1884 (BURIAL REG).

James purchased more land in Enfield, including eight meadows between Maidens Brook and the New River — Lower Mill Rounds, Upper Mill Round, Black Bush Bottom (3 plots), Olloways Meadow Carrion Pit Mead and Carrion Pit Bottom — which were added to the Forty Hall estate (ROBINSON c).

At a date between 1811 and 1815 he also acquired the manor of Honeylands and Pentriches or Capels, which on his death was inherited by his daughters, Kathleen and Mary Colvin (GLRO). For many years James Meyer was a local magistrate. When he died in 1826, at the age of 71, Forty Hall passed to his brother Herman and on his death in 1832, it went to Herman's nephew, Christian Paul Meyer. It was Christian Paul who financed the building of the nearby Jesus church which was consecrated in 1835 (KOCH). He married four times and produced nine children and it was James, a son of his first wife, to whom at the age of 22 Forty

4 James Meyer II

Hall was transferred in 1837. His father eventually retired to Brighton, where he died in 1857, although in the meantime he had rebuilt the house at Little Laver in Essex, which was to become the family seat in that county (MEYER).

Active in local affairs, James was Chairman of the Board of Magistrates as well as Chairman of the Local Board of Health from its inception in 1850 until his death in 1894. He was also Chairman of the Governors of Enfield Grammar School, Chairman of the Trustees of Enfield Charities and overseer and a churchwarden of the parish. As a young man he had commanded a troop in the Yeomanry. Elsewhere he presided over the directors of the East Middlesex Water Service and later still became Vice Chairman of the West Middlesex Water Company (OBSERVER a). He had built and maintained an infant school at Forty Hill in 1848 which lasted until an infants classroom was added to the nearby Forty Hill National School and the pupils transferred around the turn of the century; the little building still stands north of Maidens Bridge (FORD).

In 1895, Henry Carington Bowles who was living at Myddleton House purchased Forty Hall and its grounds for his eldest son Henry Ferryman Bowles, then Major but later Colonel Sir Henry Bowles, and his wife who he had married in 1889. His younger son Edward Augustus subsequently inherited Myddleton House and for many years the two estates were therefore united, not only by family ties but also physically by bridges over the old course of the New River, the common boundary between them. A great deal of renovation work and structural alterations were carried out on the house during the first six months of 1897 (GAZETTE a). Henry Ferryman Bowles was an MA of Cambridge University. He studied law and became a barrister of the Inner Temple. Commissioned into the 7th Battalion of the Rifle Brigade (Prince Consort's Own), he retired with the rank of Lieutenant Colonel. He served on the Middlesex County Council from 1889, was a Justice of the Peace and held many other public appointments as well as being chairman of innumerable local committees. Appointed Honorary Colonel of the First Volunteer Battalion of the Middlesex Regiment from 1901 to 1903, he subsequently became County Commandant during the First World War, retiring with the rank of Colonel. Active in politics he was selected as Conservative candidate for Enfield and elected as MP in 1889. Defeated by the Liberal candidate during the election of 1905 he stood again in 1918 when he was re-elected and served as MP for Enfield until 1922. Created a Baronet in 1926, he was High Sheriff for Middlesex in 1928. His interests are reflected in the fellowships he received; Royal Society of Arts, Royal Horticultural Society, the Zoological Society of London and the Marine Biological Society (GAZETTE b).

His wife, Lady Bowles, died in 1935. They had one child, Wilma, who in 1913 married Eustace Parker who in 1920 assumed the name of Bowles by Royal licence. Sir Henry Ferryman Bowles died in 1943 and was buried next to his wife in the family vault at Jesus Church. The estate was inherited by his grandson, Derek Henry Parker Bowles but burdened with ill health he was forced to sell Forty Hall and live elsewhere.

In 1951 the Forty Hall estate was purchased by the Enfield Urban District Council for £43,000 when the house was opened as a museum and the grounds became a public open space. Extensive repairs and alterations were carried out during the 1950s and 1960s and nearly every decade since.

5 Colonel Sir Henry Ferryman Bowles

2
The House — Exterior

'The MANSION HOUSE (built by Inigo Jones) is an assemblage of strength, Elegance and Convenience. And to the grand Outline of that great Artist, which appears conspicuous, are justly joined recent improvements and tasteful Embellishments ... and to the several Doors are magnificent Porticos. A Situation happily chosen; The Eminence on which it is seated, adorned with a fine Sheet of Water; the whole Ground beautifully shaped; the towering Trees appear a mass of fertile Richness' (1773)

Stucco-covered brick piers decorated with swags flank the carriage entrance and side gates at the top of Forty Hill. At their bases are cone shaped stones set firmly in the ground and intended to distance the iron-tyred wheels and metal hub covers of horse drawn vehicles turning into the gateway from the piers and prevent damage to the stucco. The wooden gates have been repaired and restored to their original design on two occasions within living memory; 1951 and again in 1996.

The present gabled lodge was designed by Sidney M Cranfield c1903. It is a well built structure; all the timber work is of oak and the roof is covered with hand made tiles (BUILDING NEWS). In the fashion of the time, the Bowles family crest and motto were placed on the front of the house. Little is known about its predecessor except that it was described in 1850 as 'handsome' (KEANE). Examination of the Breton plan and early Ordnance Survey plans show it to have been a circular building with a square-shaped extension at the rear. (BRETON AND OS. 1865 & 1896)

Inside the entrance the left fork takes the carriage drive through a belt of trees, which includes many holly trees, to the front of the house and the stables beyond, while the right fork skirts the belt of trees and the north side of the lake and continues as an approach road to the entrance of the outer courtyard and the farm buildings there. The course of either way has not changed since the end of the 18th century at least (SP PLAN) and they have probably followed the same routes since the house was built. Now tarmacadammed, the surfaces before c1951 were of gravel.

The house stands slightly to the east of the highest point of Forty Hill which, as recent excavations have confirmed, has a high water table and in consequence parts of the cellars are damp and the north lawn soon becomes waterlogged after rainfall.

Forty Hill is a remnant of the upper terrace of the River Lea where the geology is London Clay with a capping of Boyne Hill gravel. To the north, the house overlooks a broad valley with a well contained stream — Maidens Brook — which had its origin in meltwater flowing from a decaying ice sheet in the west during the Ice Age. It had demonstrably more erosive power than today which resulted in the carving out of a wide valley across which fine views can be obtained.

Several writers have stated that Forty Hall is a rebuilt version of an earlier house on the same site. It began with Lysons and his remarks under the heading 'Forty Hill', that 'Sir Nicholas Rainton became possessed of a copyhold house, described as some time Hugh Fortey's and late Sir Thomas Gurney's, quoting as his source the 1635 survey of the manor of Enfield. He goes on to say; 'This house (which has since been enfranchised) he rebuilt between the years 1629-32' (LYSONS c) . The parcel of land in question is one of many in the Forty Hill area described in various surveys as being in the possession of Sir Nicholas Rainton. The document concerned contains some interesting place names; Lane Field Grove, an unlocated tenement called Hugh Fortey's and a croft called Mayes Broadfield, and several acres of pasture known as Rush Croft, 'Öall were parcel of Hugh Fortey's since Sir Thomas Gurney, Knight'. (PRO g). Rush Croft can be identified on the Breton plan of 1785 as a plot of land about half a mile west along the lane from Forty Hall in the angle formed by the junction of the lane with the New River. Although there is nothing in the survey to indicate where Hugh Fortey's tenement stood, Lysons had obviously decided in his own mind that because of the link provided by the name, Forty Hall must have been built on the site, but there is no cartographic, documentary or archaeological evidence to support this claim. In fact the

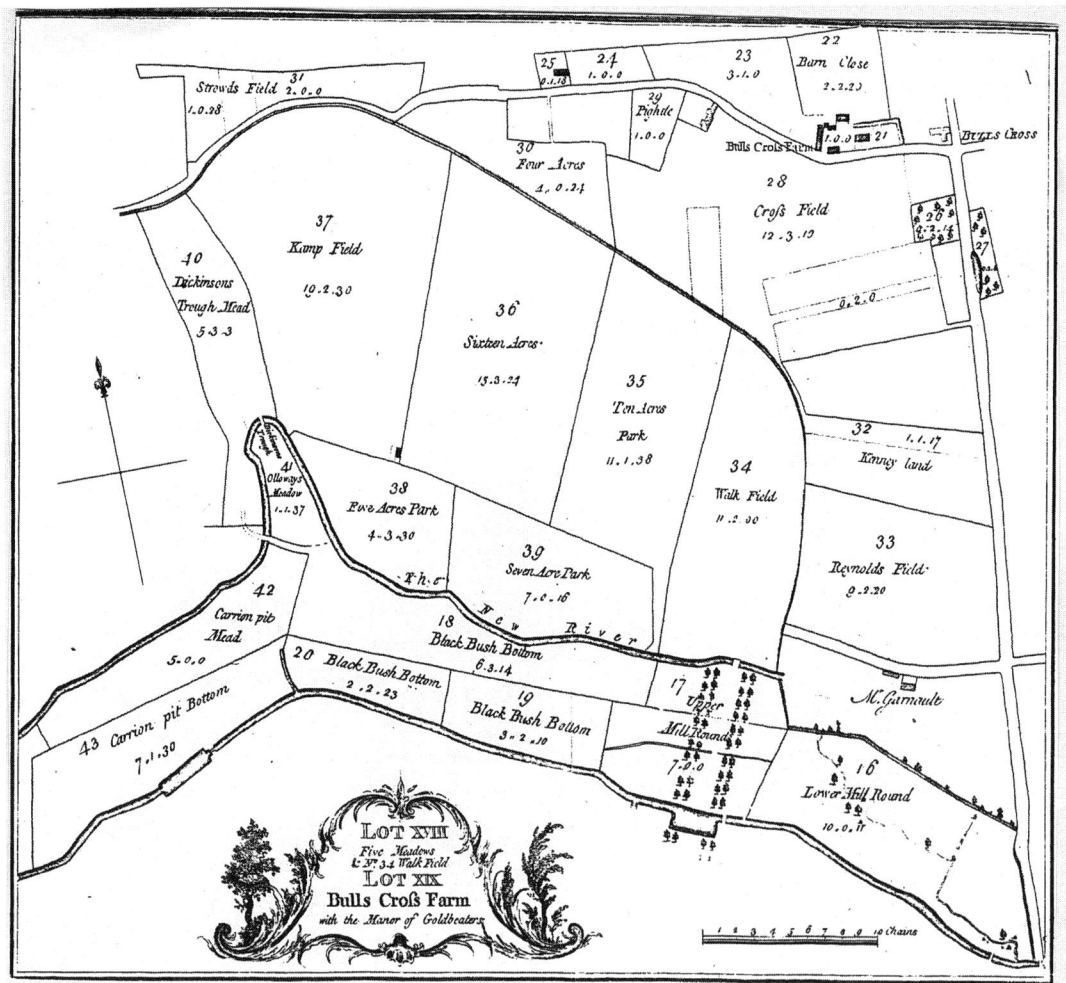
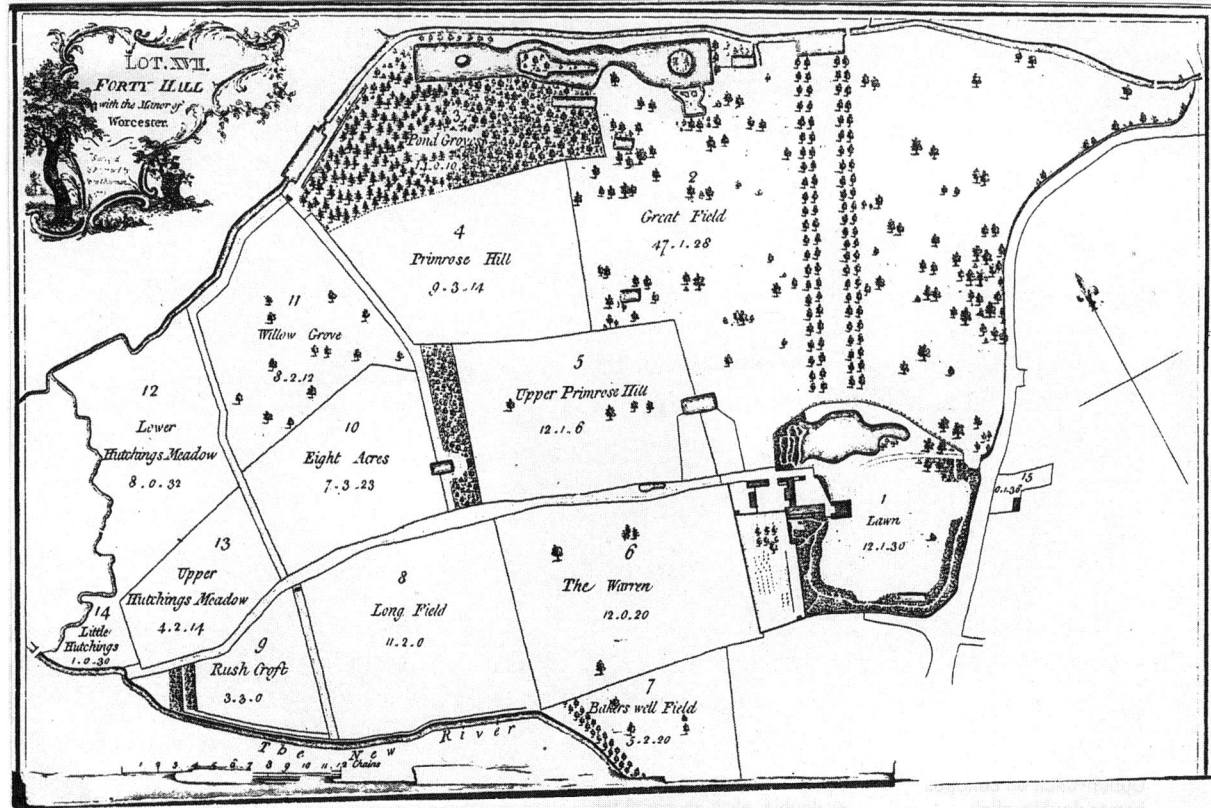

6 & 7 Plans attached to the 1773 sale catalogue

The House — Exterior

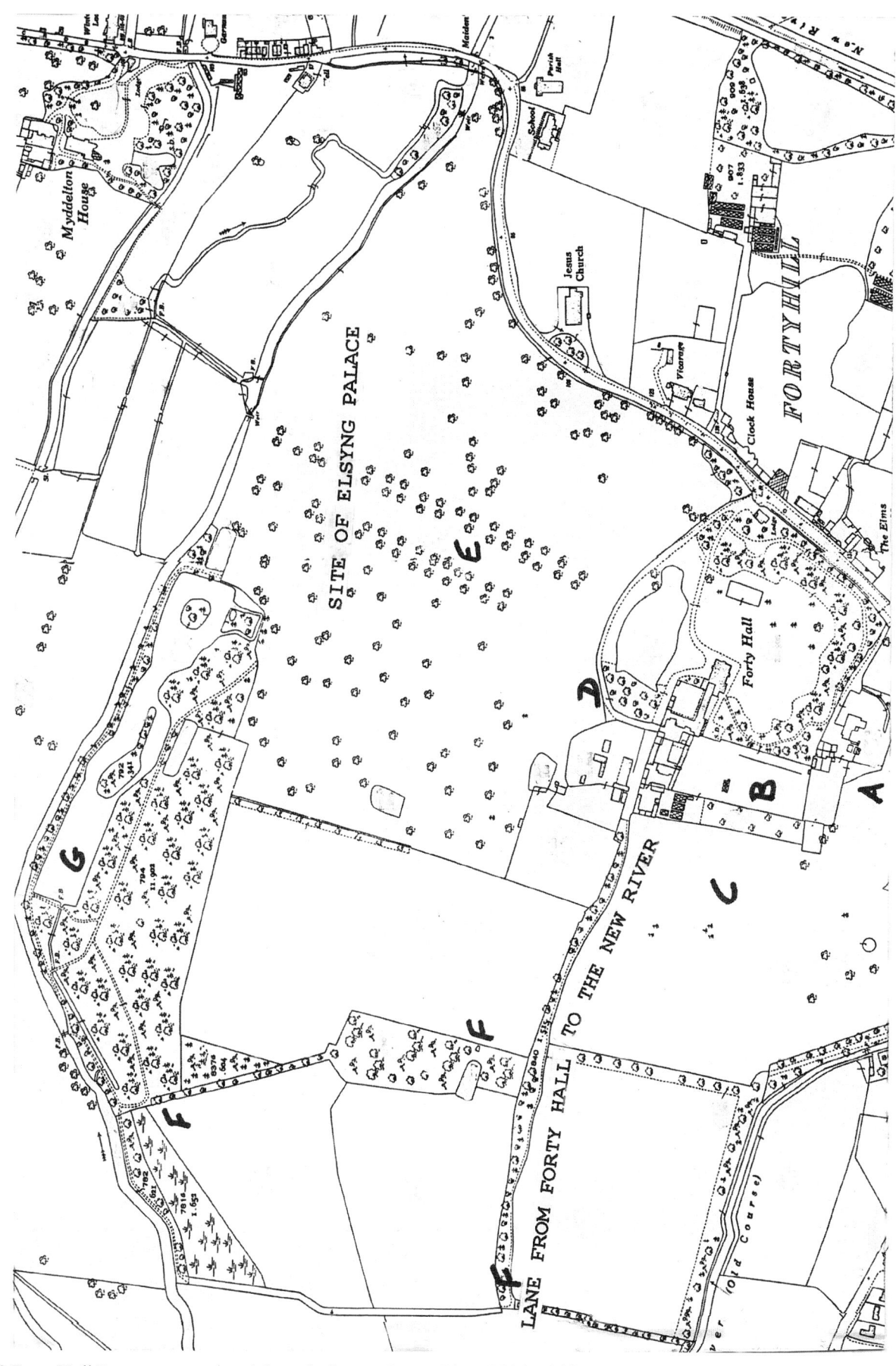

8 Forty Hall Estate — reproduced from Ordnance Survey Plans 1936 Middx II

Key: A Dower House   E Avenue of lime trees   B Walled kitchen garden   F Sites of summerhouses
       C Warren field   G Lower lake   D Garden mount

name of the present house must come from the hill on which it stood — even here there is confusion as one or two writers exercised their imaginations and saw the name of Forty Hill as a corruption of Four Tree Hill (ROBINSON d) for which there is no evidence whatsoever. There was a Richard Atte Fortye who held land in 1340 (PRO h) and both Forty Hill and Forty Green were in use as place names in 1572 (PRO I).

Exterior

The house is a square compact block of elegant design with symmetrical facades containing carefully proportioned rectangular windows with broad flat surrounds set on raised brickwork — all the present window surrounds were replaced during restoration work in the 1950s or 1960s. There is banding between each of the three storeys and rusticated cement angles or quoins. Centrally placed porches occupy the north, east and south sides. It has a slate covered hipped roof with octagonal, square or concave sided shafts of the chimney stacks, all of which have been heavily restored or in some cases completely rebuilt, such as the north-west stack which in 1894 had four flues (P1894) but was later rebuilt (c1897) with only three.

Although large quantities of bricks were occasionally moved over long distances even before adequate transport facilities became available, it made economic sense to locate a suitable source of clay as close as possible to the site of the proposed house where bricks could be made. It is known that land at Clay Hill involved in a conveyance dated 1594 was described as 'abutting north-west on the old tile-kilns' (ROBINSON e). These are believed to be the kilns which provided tiles and bricks for Elsyng Palace (PALACES a) and there seems little doubt that a few years later these same kilns were again producing bricks, this time for the construction of Forty Hall.

Subsequent erosion, especially at the east corner of the north side of the house, has exposed the internal structure of some of the hand made bricks, which at this point are laid in an irregular bond. Some of the

9 View of Forty Hill, Enfield Middlesex, Seat of James Meyer, Esq

10 Forty Hill from the Goat public house, looking north c1900

11 Entrance gates to Forty Hall

12 Lodge, side view

13 Lodge, Front view

14 Front view of house 1894

brickwork around the north porch appears to have been renewed, perhaps when the stucco was removed in 1897, as the bricks there are of much better quality and look as if they were machine made. They are laid in Flemish bond — alternate headers and stretchers in each course. The brickwork of the upper storeys is also for the most part laid in Flemish bond. Brickwork on the east and south sides, although irregular, does appear to be a form of English bond; alternate courses of headers and stretchers with one distinct exception. Between the east side of the south porch and the nearby window frame the area of brickwork from the line of the lower window sill to the banding between the ground and first floors is laid in perfect Flemish bond. Flemish bond was introduced into this country during the first half of the 17th century and Kew Palace built in 1631 is often cited as the first use of this pattern. However, there were many variations of Flemish bond (and for that matter of English Bond) and the evidence of the brickwork at Forty Hall suggests it was laid during the transition from English to Flemish bond. It is not uncommon for both examples and their variants to be seen in other houses; Cromwell House at Highgate and Raynham Hall in Norfolk are two examples (CLIFTON TAYLOR), and as already suggested, allowance has to be made for the subsequent renewal of parts of the brickwork for various reasons from time to time.

A moulded brick bearing the date 1629 can be seen just above ground level on the front of the house near the north-east corner and records the year in which building work began. Near the top of the building there was once another brick bearing the date 1632 (GOUGH) indicating the year of completion of the house, but this too has gone.

The small north-west wing was added in 1636, dated by an incised brick, and the sharp angle of the south-east corner has been cut back, leaving a corbelled overhang at first floor level. The door on the front of this extension was originally at the north-west corner at the end of the present corridor and moved to its present position during alterations in the 1950s or 1960s. Another slightly larger wing at the south-west corner of the house may also have been added during the first half of the 17th century (RCHM). The exterior brickwork of the north side of the upper storey is much later but, as in the case of parts of the north front of the house, this was probably part of the replacement of damaged or eroded bricks following the removal of stucco in 1897. Unfortunately, pebble dash has covered up details of the brickwork of the ground floor. On the outside wall of this wing is a metal frame containing a bell once used to summon estate workers — no doubt on pay day and on other occasions. High up on the wall of the house, between the two extensions, is a brick, a stretcher, with the initials AN, perhaps those of a builder. The extensions break the symmetrical design of the house and the only reason that springs to mind for their construction is that when the house was completed in 1632 it was found that insufficient space had been allocated for service rooms.

There is a traditional but mistaken belief that Inigo Jones was the architect responsible for the building

15 Rear of house 1894

of Forty Hall. Apart from one possible exception, there is no private country house that can be firmly established as the work of Jones, although he did collaborate with other architects from time to time whose work was often influenced by his designs. A good case has been made for Edward Carter, Chief Clerk to the King's Works, as the architect of Forty Hall. Carter worked for a time with Jones, who he succeeded as Surveyor-General, but he developed an individual astylar manner which he applied to several houses in this country (HARRIS).

It was at one time believed that hipped roofs did not appear until a little later than 1629 and that Forty Hall had been built with a series of plain straight sided gables on each side of the roof as at Boston Manor, near Brentford — 1622-23 or, alternatively, with curved gable ends and top pediments as displayed at Swakeleys, near Ickenham — 1629-38 (PEVSNER). Recent opinion, however, takes the view that as the existing hipped roof at Forty Hall contains mostly re-used timbers it could not have been replaced in c1700 as once believed and must therefore be original (McGUIRE). This being so, the house is one of advanced design and an early and important example of its kind (WORSLEY).

Externally, the appearance of the house has been considerably altered during the intervening years. We are told that Forty Hall was repaired and modernised by Wolstenholme in the year 1700 which would be about the time the block modillion cornice, which covers most of the top storey window surrounds, was fitted and earlier casement windows, with their mullions and transoms, were replaced by the fashionable new sash windows. This is an event recorded in an entry in the margin of the Richard Gough's notes about the house when he states; 'it first had two bow windows on each side which were taken away by Nicholas Wolstenholme' (GOUGH). Was Gough referring to bow windows or bay windows? In any event, his remarks add to the evidence for the many changes made to the appearance of the house. The east entrance was probably inserted and the three porches added at about the same time as the windows were replaced. These alterations may have been carried out in 1708 when rainwater heads endorsed W(Wolstenholme?) over the letters G M (architect or builder?) were installed (ROBINSON f)

One of the bricks used in the construction of a 17th century garden wall found during excavations by the Enfield Archaeological Society on the north lawn in 1993 had a moulded groove across one end. This provided evidence for the method of construction of the original sills for the earlier casement windows of the house, with bricks of this type laid side by side and the groove forming a drip channel beneath the overhanging edge. Later in the 18th century, during the tenure of Edmund Armstrong, the walls of the

16 Front and east view of Forty Hall, 1932

house were covered in white stucco (GOUGH). A watercolour of Forty Hall dated 1793 (DAYES) shows the front elevation, north lawn and the lake. Also included in the scene are, a large marquee beneath the cedar tree on the east side of the house, a man on horseback and a scaled down version of a galleon on the surface of the lake. It is reminiscent of a fete champetre; the re-creation of an historical event — a presentation very popular at this time — but no guess can be made regarding the significance of the event portrayed. Rainwater heads on the front and rear elevations carry the initials of James Meyer and the date 1800.

Further alterations to the exterior of the house were made by the Bowles family in 1897 with the insertion of large landing windows in the east elevation and the removal of the decayed and now unfashionable stucco from the brickwork (OBSERVER b). A canopy supported on slim metal columns which stood against the east side of the house was removed at the same time (P 1894)

More work was carried out after the purchase of the house by Enfield Urban District Council in 1951 — mention has already been made of the re-located door in the north-west extension — and public lavatories were added near the north-west corner of the house.

The north front contains the main entrance to the house. Originally a double door, the two leaves, each with raised panels, were bolted together c1951 to form a single door. The impost and arch are decorated with scroll ornament and above is a semi-circular fanlight covered with wood tracery. Doric columns and pilasters of the porch support an entablature in the centre of which are two doves in plaster relief and a single dove on top of each pilaster. There is a segmented pediment containing a blank cartouche surrounded by foliage decoration with half pediments at each side. The glass screens and door between the columns are modern additions. A domed ceiling has narrow moulded ribs or groins and a moulded plaster leaf ornament in the centre. The floor has been re-paved in recent years. Fastened to the wall of the house above the north porch are two fire marks of the Sun Fire Office. The one at the top is endorsed with insurance policy 173711 dated 12th February 1760 and gives details of insurance against loss or damage by fire at Forty Hall between Eliab Breton and the 'Society of the Sun Fire Office' in London (POLICYa).

17 Rear of house c1980

18 View of house and lake from the north

Beneath is an earlier fire mark bearing insurance policy number 12591 dated 14th November 1718, which was taken out by 'William Frederick Lord Hunsdon of Albemarle Street, the parish of St. Martins in the Fields for his new Dwelling House only at Forty Hill in the parish of Enfield'. Succeeding policies, 12592 and 12593, gave insurance cover 'for his outhouses' and 'for his goods in the said house'. (POLICY b).

The double leaf doors of the east entrance have been retained, each with three raised panels, and there is a semi-circular fanlight covered with wood tracery contained in an arch supported by plain imposts with leaf scroll ornament in the spandrels. The porch has Ionic columns and pilasters, the capitals decorated with swags, supporting an entablature similar to the one on the north porch but with a winged cherub's head in the centre. There is a segmented pediment bearing a cartouche, identical to the one of the north porch, which once contained the arms of the Wolstenholme family, later removed by Armstrong (GOUGH), and there were once half pediments at each side (P 1894) but these were removed during the insertion of the landing windows in 1897. The ceiling is also similar to the one in the north porch and decorated in the same fashion. Stone slabs with black diamond-shaped insets at the corners which cover the floor were probably laid in 1897, at the same time as the terrace at the rear of the house was built and where the same sort of stone occurs.

On the south side of the house there is an entrance with a double-height door and window surround. Tuscan columns and pilasters support an entablature and a ceiling with a design similar to the other porches. Above the porch two fluted Corinthian columns support an entablature and a triangular pediment. Pilaster strips in the form of cement rendering on each side of the upper storey window continue the line of the door and window surround columns to the eaves cornice which projects slightly between their width. A single door and glass screens to the porch, as well as the glazing within the window surround are modern. In fact, the whole assembly above the porch may also be a later addition and the porch itself may have had pediments similar to the other porches, later modified to its present form.

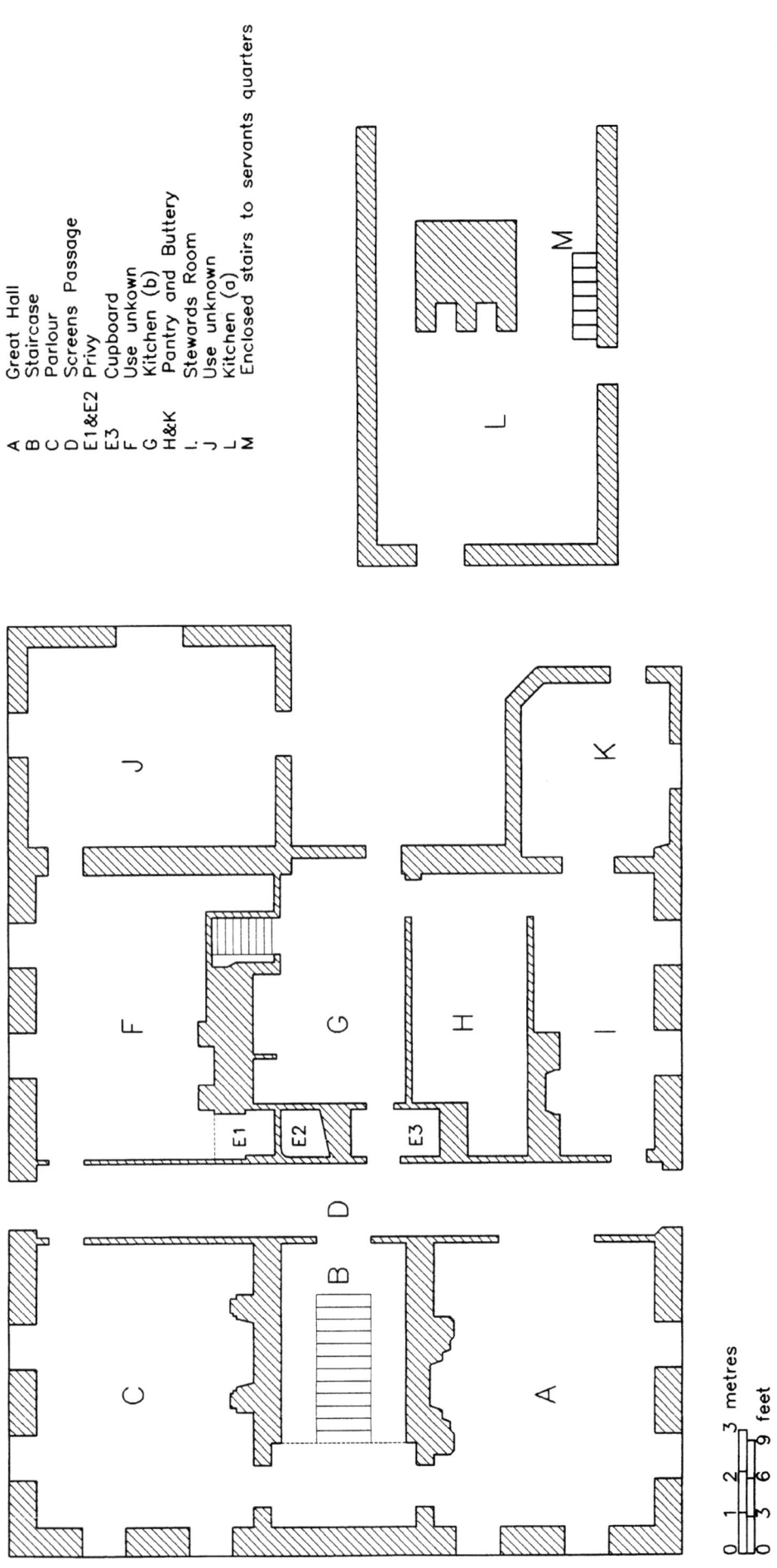

19 *Conjectural plan of house 1629-32 with extensions J and K added in 1636*

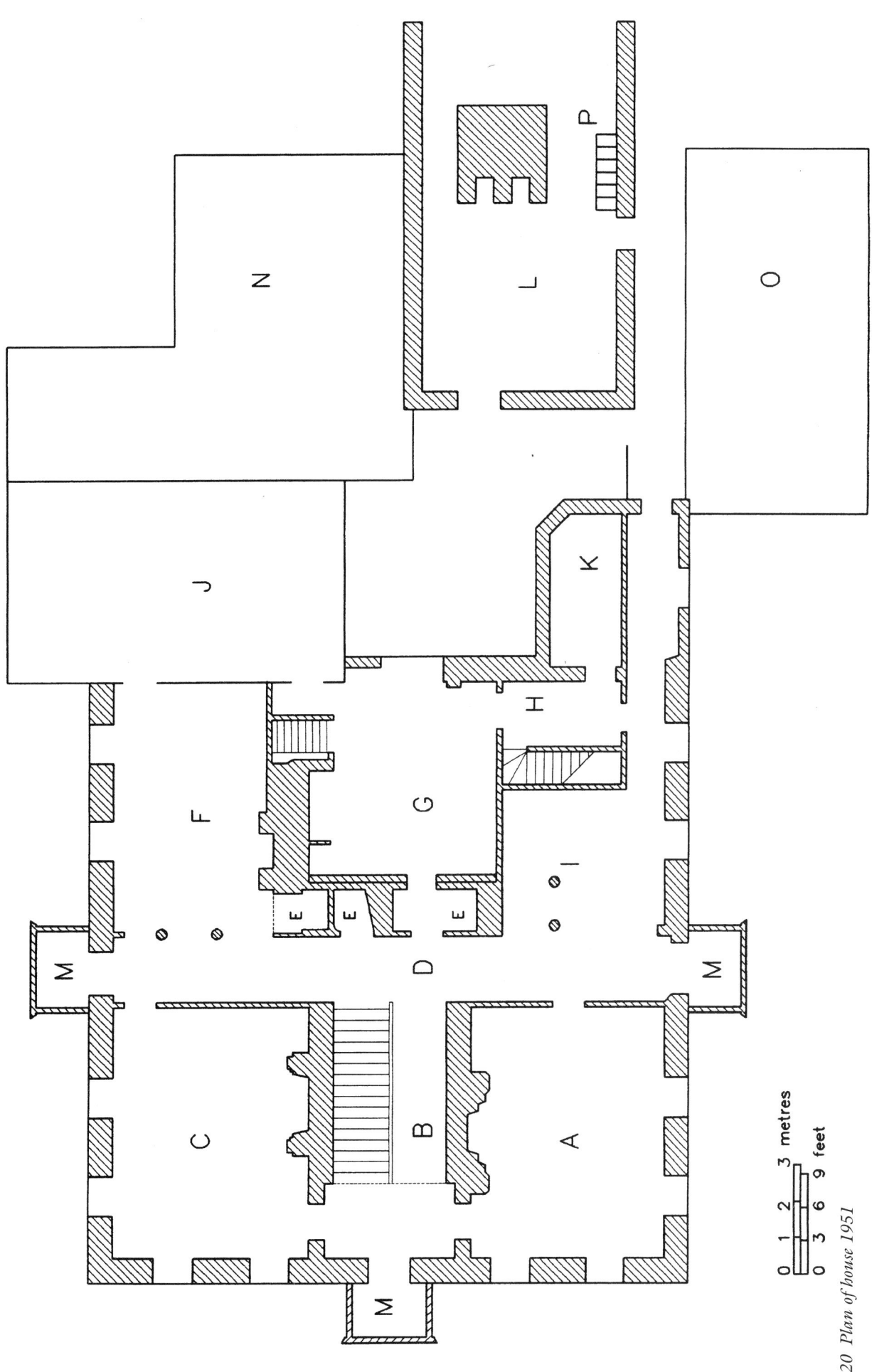

20 Plan of house 1951

3
The House — Interior

'The FIRST FLOOR comprehends a Drawing Room, Dining and Breakfasting Parlour, and Study; These Apartments are arranged in well concerted Order, elegantly proportioned, and suberbly decorated; the Singularity and Boldness of the Original Ornaments are ingeniously opposed to the petite Neatness of the present' (1773)

Great Hall

A passage from the main entrance to the garden door at the rear divides the house between the grand rooms on the left and the service rooms on the right. To the left of the main door is the Great Hall; a medieval concept which continued to be included in the designs of houses into the 17th century, and was used for receptions and other formal occasions. It is separated from the passage by a good example of a 17th century screen, the central arched opening of which was blocked by the present doorway and surround during the 18th century. The screen has pilaster flanked bays each divided vertically into three parts; at the top is a scallop shell design, in the central panel is a raised strapped oval and below is a raised design in the form of a double arcaded window. Each of the pilaster columns is topped with busts of semi-grotesque heads; two bearded men and two women, above is a decorated frieze and cornicing. The spandrels of the original arch contain cherub heads. The 18th century decoration filling the arch consist of another large scallop shell above the door, to match the earlier examples on either side, with symmetrical mouldings in the remaining spaces.

Apart from the later inner marble surround, the fireplace, of wood, is original. Flanking pilasters are decorated with bandwork and terminate in a shelf surmounted by a moulded square panel enclosing a decorated cartouche with a gabled pediment. On either side there is scrollwork decorated with cherub heads flanked by obelisk designs, a notable Jacobean motif symbolising prestige and power. The cartouche once contained the arms of the Wolstenholme and Rainton families but these were removed by Armstrong c1788 (GOUGH).

The ceiling with its geometrical design, together with other decorated ceilings on this side of the house, is original and believed to be the work of Edward Stanyon, d1631 (GAPPER). The design for each ceiling was prefabricated and laid out on the floor before being lifted and plastered into place. When dry, they would have been painted white.

Wood panelling, originally plain, but later painted white, which lines the lower part of the walls, although thought to be of 17th century date, may have been re-modelled subsequent to its original installation (HARWOOD). This may have been done by Edmund Armstrong when he converted the room from a formal reception area into a 'parlour' as part of the renovations to the property on which he spent £4,000 in c1788. Previously Eliab Breton had continued the tradition of earlier owners by using this room as a formal reception area for occasions such as entertaining their tenants once a year (ROBINSON f). It eventually became the family dining room. The internal window shutters in this and other rooms of the house are much later replacements.

Key to Fig 20 (overleaf)
A   *Great hall*
B   *Main staircase, rebuilt c1708 and 1897*
C   *Drawing room*
D   *Screens passage*
E   *Cupboards*
F   *Pillar room c1760, Rainton Room 1951*
G   *Kitchen from c1800*
H   *Back stairs, inserted c1708*
I   *Reception, created during the 18th century; plaster decoration applied c1760*
J   *Extended and rebuilt 1897*
K   *Butler's pantry, c1708*
L   *Original kitchen 1632-c1800*
M   *Porches and east entrance, added c1708*
N   *Additions of c1800 and 1897 (in outline only)*
O   *Servant's hall, built 1928 (in outline only)*
P   *Enclosed stairs to servants' quarters*

21 Screen in Great Hall

22 Fireplace in Great Hall

23 Main staircase

Staircase Passage

Next to the Great Hall is the staircase passage leading to the east door. The large arched entrance to the passage and main staircase was created by the removal of brickwork when the staircase was rebuilt in its present form at the end of the 19th century (OBSERVER b). Twisted balusters incorporated in the remodelled staircase are typical of those in use in c1700 (ALCOCK AND HALL), which implies that the original staircase was replaced at the beginning of the 18th century before being reconstructed yet again in 1897. Nothing is known about these earlier staircases. The only reference we have is the 1773 sale catalogue, which states that; 'The Staircases are centrically placed'. However, this may indicate the type of staircase that existed prior to 1897; a single flight rising from the middle of the stairwell direct to a mezzanine floor extending round all four sides at first floor level, with a similarly constructed flight to the second floor. Evidence for the re-alignment of the staircase can be seen on both landings where cracks in the plaster on opposing walls reveal the outlines of former doorways. In the room over the Great Hall, one of the door frames is still in situ with the sill about two feet higher than the present first floor landing. It can also be seen that the insertion of this landing has obscured part of the fanlight over the door of the east entrance. It is therefore obvious that earlier landings were at the same level as the floors they served.

From the landing, three steps lead up to the first floor level and a cross passage giving access to bedrooms and dressings rooms on either side of the house. A second identical flight of stairs leads to the top landing and the attic bedrooms. Above is an ornate plaster ceiling. It has a central oval panel surrounded by a strapwork design with a deep frieze decorated in the same fashion.

The canopied ceiling shows that the staircase originally occupied much less space than it does today, each flight rising at a very steep angle, perhaps as much as 30 degrees. The restricted areas on each side of the first flight may have inhibited access, and for this reason and the evidence of the first floor fenestration, it is believed that the east entrance, as well as the porch, was not constructed until the early 18th century —

c1708. Stairs were rarely carpeted until the early 19th century.

The large window inserted on the first floor landing in 1897 is divided into four sections which contain the arms of the Bowles and other families linked to them by marriage or tradition and these are described in appendix one.

South-East (Drawing) Room

Beyond the staircase passage is another ornately decorated room on the ground floor which later became the drawing room. It is clad in good undisturbed 17th century panelling now painted white but like that in the rest of the house originally plain. There is a plaster ceiling with another geometrical design with rosettes in plasterwork contained in a moulded ribbed pattern and a centrally placed cartouche and blank shield, both of which would once have contained painted arms. Although it, too, has been reduced in size by the insertion of a marble surround, the fireplace is original.. Pairs of half round Doric columns supporting a shelf and a two-bayed over-mantle which also has pairs of Doric columns flanking the bays, each of which contains a raised strapped oval inside a square panel, with an entablature above.

24 Fireplace in south-east (drawing) room

Steward's Room, Buttery & Pantry

'The Hall adorned with a screen of columns. Mosaic Pavement, and elaborate Designs in Stucco....' (1773)

The 'Hall' referred to in the 1773 sale catalogue must be the present open reception area to the right of the main entrance, once occupied by the Steward's room, and created by removing part of the screens passage wall, a fireplace and chimney flue and replacing the latter with unfluted Ionic columns and a ceiling beam to support the brickwork above. Plasterwork decoration on the walls consists of ribbed panels some containing swags and others with musical instruments, actors' masks, sheet music and foliage in plaster relief. The notation displayed on the plaster representations of sheet music was examined by members of the

25 Ceiling in south-east (drawing) room

26 Present reception, formerly steward's room

London College of Music but it could not be identified as any part of a recognisable musical score. Four medallions each consisting of a head within circular ribbed surrounds were claimed, unconvincingly, by a previous writer to represent the seasons (GUIDE). On the south wall are three arches; the open arch on the left contains the screens passage, in the central blind arch is an apsidal recess with an inverted scallop shell design at the top, and the third arch, also blind, contains plaster decoration similar to that elsewhere on the walls. Plaster heads in relief appear at the top of the left and right hand arches with a plaster modillion above the central arch. A plaster head identical to the others appears over the back of the arched fanlight of the main door. The ceiling beam and cornicing are also heavily decorated and there is raised leaf decoration in the centre of the ceiling, within which is a modern light fitting. A similar light fitting can be seen in the ceiling of the screens passage.

The type of plaster decoration displayed in the reception area was fashionable from the 1720's until the 1760's (REID). Medallions containing heads in profile were popular throughout this period but the introduction of music and wind instruments as part of internal plasterwork came after 1750 (WARE, BEARD). No traces remain of the 'Mosaic Pavements' but it is assumed they once covered the floor of the present reception area and were installed during the second half of the 18th century. It is suggested that Eliab Breton was responsible for the alterations to this part of the house and the application of the decorative plasterwork in the present reception area, the screen passage and the Rainton room. Work which would have led him to consider insuring his house which, as we have seen, he did in 1760 with the Sun Fire Office.

The floors of most of the downstairs rooms are of good quality narrow boarded timber, matching those on the staircase landings and were probably laid in c1897, although the linoleum on the floor of the drawing room only dates from c1960. Flagstones cover the floor of the north-west wing, the area in which the backstairs are situated, and the adjoining corridor. The middle room has a parquet floor laid c1960 on a solid base which may also have once consisted of flagstones. Originally, only the main reception rooms would have had carpets on the floor, with rush matting being used elsewhere.

The steward was responsible for the administration and smooth running of the household and his room would have been situated in the most strategic position, which in this case was at the front of the house, close to the screens passage and the main entrance. Nearby would have been the pantry and the buttery where supplies of food and drink were stored, for which the steward was also responsible; most of the space in the north-west wing, and in the adjoining room, later occupied by the back stairs, would have been used for this purpose.

Beyond the west wall of the reception area are the back stairs, the shape of the balusters c1700 being the same as those in the later, remodelled, main staircase. The back stairs have probably remained unaltered since they were first installed, perhaps as part of the previously described alterations carried out in 1708. The insertion of these stairs into a relatively small space was an awkward arrangement as shown by the shape and angles of the treads and the way in which the staircase ignores pre-existing features.

In the wall next to the backstairs was an arched opening blocked during the 1950s, which had earlier provided a means of communication between the middle room beyond — later to become the kitchen — the back stairs and the nearby north-west wing. Part of the north-west wing subsequently became a butler's pantry and the remainder forms a corridor from the reception to the end of the wing where an outside door once stood. This as we have seen was removed, post 1951, and inserted into a new doorway cut for the purpose in the nearby north wall.

Middle Room

Although the downstairs middle room was in use as a kitchen when the representatives from the Royal Commission of Historical Monuments visited Forty Hall in 1937, they endorsed the traditional belief that the old scullery and kitchen at the eastern end of the south range of courtyard buildings were original (RCHM).

In the early 17th century many kitchens were still detached buildings at a sufficient distance from the house to reduce the risk of fire and prevent the smells of cooking permeating other rooms. The original purpose of the downstairs middle room was probably where cooked food was brought by kitchen staff for preparation before being collected and served by servants who waited at table. The room has a solid floor and in the west wall there is a blocked up fireplace which would have had cupboards beside it where food could be kept warm. Although modern pebble dash on the exterior has obscured the outline of the known doorway in the east wall of the former kitchen, stonework in the surface of the yard marks its former position. A similar feature beneath the window of the middle room opposite also indicates the position of an earlier doorway, since converted into a window. This direct means of communication reduced to a few steps the distance cooked food had to be carried to the warming cupboards and at the same time sufficient distance was maintained between the two buildings for the reasons previously mentioned.

Cooking arrangements were eventually transferred to the middle room. Although it is uncertain when this was done it unlikely to have been until some time during the 18th century when the kitchen range became available. Even so this type of range still required the use of spits, cranes and other paraphernalia necessary for open fire cooking and it more likely that any improvements in cooking facilities would have been confined to modification of the existing arrangements in the original kitchen. It was not until the beginning of the 19th century that the more efficient closed range was invented and one such piece of equipment was no doubt introduced into Forty Hall and the cooking arrangements then re-located. We know that the transfer took place before 1823 as William Robinson writing in the early years of the 19th century refers to the incised brick dated 1636 as 'being near the kitchen window', once a doorway (ROBINSON g). So, perhaps it was James, the first member of the Meyer family to live at Forty Hall, 1799-1824, who made the transfer. It may have been at this time that the eastern, timber-framed, wall of the middle room was lined with brick, no doubt as a precaution against fire. The range would in turn have been replaced with a gas cooker after the production of an efficient gas appliance in the 1870s; the pipework of the old gas main was found during excavations on the north lawn in 1993 but the date of its installation is not known. In the south-east corner of the middle room a door conceals a flight of wooden steps leading to the basement.

South-West (Rainton) Room

Following the construction of the adjoining wing, c1636, a doorway was inserted in the wall of the south-west room to allow communication between them. Part of the mid 18th century alterations involved the removal of the passage wall to enlarge this room. The wall was replaced by an open screen consisting of two columns supporting a ceiling high arch, lintels and a deep plain frieze with cornicing similar to that in the

27 South-west (Rainton) room

reception area and along the screens passage. A door was fitted across the truncated line of the passage with a fanlight above containing decorative metal work and surmounted by a plaster head. The enlarged room was known from this time as the Pillar Room and later on, after 1951, it became the Rainton Room.

A portrait of Sir Nicholas Rainton dated 1643, described in an early guide as probably the work of William Dobson, a pupil of Van Dyke (GUIDE) but said by Richard Gough to be an original painting by C Jansson, forms an overmantle. The fact that only part of his coat of arms can be seen in the top right hand corner shows that the picture was originally much larger and was probably cut down to fit its present location. The fireplace has a wide-shouldered architrave with entablature and this and the chimney breasts around the portrait are decorated with swags and foliage in low plaster relief. Today, they are painted in a variety of colours but originally they would have been in only one colour — white. The ceiling and walls, apart from the cornicing, are plain.

There was cupboard in the far corner of the room on the same side as the chimney breast but this was later blocked, c1897, and converted into a passage between the kitchen in the middle room and a newly-constructed scullery in the south-west wing. To the right of the fireplace is a recessed area forming another cupboard, on the inside of the door of which are pencilled the names of the Meyer and Bowles family children and their friends. The Bowles children were measured yearly and their heights recorded against the door. The interior, which has been fitted with shelves, suggests that as was often the case elsewhere it had once housed a privy.

The front half of the cupboard, the lower part of which is clad in match-board of 19th century date, rises to the height of the ceiling of the adjoining room and the floor is boarded over the earth below. At the rear, offsets in the brickwork indicate the ends of the parallel walls of the east wall of the middle room and the west wall of the screens passage. The space between them is occupied by two solid brick constructions now in use as cupboards but thought at one time to have been a privy and a chute to a cess pit beneath the house — the equivalent of a medieval garderobe often constructed within the thickness of the walls of the building concerned. Part of the angled brickwork of the former chute can be seen at the base of the recessed rear wall where it slopes back and down at an angle of about 20 degrees. This was a system which persisted well into the 19th century and, lacking a nearby river or convenient moat into which contents could be discharged, many of these cess pits would need to be emptied from time to time. However, there are examples where they were sealed after the body of a dead animal has been placed within: the consequential biological action would ensure that the organic material in the cesspit would be consumed (HUNSDON). Any attempt to locate such a cesspit would require excavations beneath the central part of the house.

The configuration of the brickwork inside the cupboard in the Rainton Room and the adjoining space beyond, which was also later converted into a cupboard by inserting a door into the screens passage wall opposite the foot of the main staircase, suggests that a second privy may have been installed upstairs. However, there has been considerable re-modelling of the landing passage on the first floor, probably when the staircase was rebuilt in 1897, which has obliterated all traces of earlier structures in the area concerned.

In order to maintain the symmetry of the screens passage, the line of the west wall was continued, this time in lath and plaster construction, to the end of the former steward's room. The wall is pierced by a door opposite the staircase passage, behind which another door opens into the middle room. The small recesses on either side are, and probably always have been, used as cupboards. An examination of the wall within the enclosed area located the timber upright which supported the ceiling beam of the original north wall of the middle room and beside it there is at least one timber stud still in place; the removal of the modern plaster and wallpaper would probably reveal others.

Servants' Hall

The cartographic evidence shows that between the late 18th and the mid 19th century, a small extension had been built on the front of the north-west wing (SP PLAN, OS 1865). In 1927 it was demolished to make way for a larger extension which abutted the north-west corner of the 1636 wing, intended for use as a servants hall. Bricks used in its construction came from the recently demolished Old Rectory in Chase Side (RCHM). Since 1951 it has provided accommodation for museum staff. The servants hall encroached on the south-east corner of the inner courtyard and extended the corridor on this side of the house to its present length and a door was placed at the courtyard end.

Staff were still accommodated in the attic storey but in addition the butler and footman had rooms over the old kitchen and scullery in the south range of the courtyard buildings, from 1924 onwards at least.

After the Civil War, 1642 — 1649, the younger sons of gentlemen no longer entered houses as stewards or pages. As a result there was a decline in the social status of servants with yeoman instead of gentlemen becoming stewards. Butlers eventually took over the responsibility for managing the pantry and buttery with other servants performing duties elsewhere in the house. By the 19th century there were clear social distinctions between all classes and this extended to the ranks of servants where a rigid hierarchy often prevailed.

Although the ten year census returns between 1841 and 1891 give some information about the domestic staff at Forty Hall, they only include those members who were there on the night of the census. Some servants lived out, and there would be others who were with members of the family on visits elsewhere — there would also be servants of visitors to Forty Hall. The occupations listed in the various census returns include; cook and housekeeper, housemaids, children's maid, kitchen maid, under-housemaid, scullery maid, footmen, coachmen, grooms and in 1861 a 14 year old page. Only one servant was resident at Forty Hall for more than 10 years between 1841 and 1891; Mary Richards, housekeeper in 1851 at the age of 60 was still there when the next census was taken in 1861.

In later years, from c1924 until the Second World War, the indoor staff consisted of; a butler, footman — in 1924 there were two footmen but this number was later reduced to one — lady's maid, three housemaids, cook/housekeeper, kitchen maid and a scullery maid. Outdoors there was a chauffeur, handyman, two carpenters, painter, head gardener and several assistant gardeners, a cowman, farm hands and a gamekeeper. A gardener, who continued to work there after Enfield Council had purchased the estate, lived out in one of the houses (SCHEDULE) owned by Colonel Bowles in St. Georges Road at the foot of Forty Hall.

In the angle formed by the south-west extension and the wall of the scullery and kitchen was added another extension built between 1773 and 1865, containing a small room and a separate kitchen for use by the housekeeper.

Late in the 19th century the south-west wing was extended by adding a large bay window; the enlarged area was then divided into two by erecting a wall containing a fireplace for each of the two new rooms thus created. Cornices and large panels with varied mouldings of early 18th century date decorated the original room. The larger of the two rooms was used as a parlour and the other became a scullery. Connection of the latter with the middle room, which by now had become the kitchen was effected by cutting a doorway through the intervening wall and converting an adjoining cupboard into a short communicating passage. This was the cupboard which originally opened into the south-west room, the door of which was then blocked and the back removed to provide the necessary access. It was in its turn sealed off during renovation work in the 1950s. A small utility room and WC were added in c1895 together with entry into an existing passage and the provision of a new rear entrance.

First Floor

'... the principal Bedchambers and Dressing Rooms, which there are ten, are pleasant, commodious, and neatly embellished' (1773).

The north-east room, over the Great Hall, is lined with raised and fielded panelling of the early 18th century, separated by a moulded dado rail. There are three doorways, two of which are blocked; one once led to the first floor landing and the other into the adjoining room. The fireplace has a moulded surround of black and variegated marble. There is an original plaster ceiling with a design of square cornered and interlacing quatrefoils outlined with ribbed panels containing scroll and jewelled arabesque designs. A moulded cornice surrounds the ceiling.

The south-east room over the drawing room has early 18th century panelling, cornice and doors similar to those of the north-east room although the moulding of the panels on the walls is slightly different. The fireplace, with a plain marble surround with a narrow moulded edge, is placed diagonally across the corner of the room — not unknown but still a curious and unexplained arrangement, which may be a later modification as the chimney flue for fireplaces in the rooms above and below are aligned directly on the chimney breast in the centre of the north wall. An elaborately decorated ceiling is made up of squares and rectangles, the latter having quadrant corners arranged alternately round a square, placed diagonally and including four quadrant ribs. These ribs are the same shape in section and the panels also contain similar designs to those in the north-east rooms. One of the panels contain the date 1629 but the rest of the space, now blank, would once have contained a coat of arms. The position of this dated panel shows it must have been intended to be the centre of a much longer room which included all or part of the

28 Ceiling in north-east room on the first floor

29 Dated ceiling in south-east room on the first floor

adjoining lobby previously created by erecting a partition to separate it into two rooms, and by building a cupboard or walk-in wardrobe nearby in c1897. That part of the decorated ceiling once within the present lobby has been removed but a remnant of the decoration can still be seen inside the adjoining cupboard or wardrobe. However, it is not immediately apparent why the panel in question was not centrally placed in relation to the width of the room. Opposite the cupboard or wardrobe is a doorway inserted c1897 or later after a bath had been installed in the present annexe and this new doorway provided access to the adjoining bedroom when the bathroom was in use. The doorway was blocked during alterations c1951.

The room over the main entrance with north facing windows also has 18th century panelling and a cornice identical to the rooms over the Great Hall and the Drawing Room with doors and fireplaces also of similar design..

The construction of the room over the north-west wing c1636 may also date from the 17th century but the present interior is quite plain with modern plastered walls and ceiling. In later years, it was used as the nursery kitchen and laundry. This wing had an external chimney stack with a single flue at the north-west corner and there appears to have been another at the south-west corner. The only evidence for these features comes from a late 19th century photograph (P 1894).

In the north-west corner of the original house was a small room the original purpose of which is not known but part of it was used c1708 to accommodate the second flight of the back stairs. A WC was later, c1897, fitted into the small remaining space between the wall of the backstairs and the north-west extension. It probably replaced an earlier earth closet.

Overlooking the enclosed yard, the upstairs middle room, used as a study or business room as it became known and later on as a store room, has walls lined with original panelling of the 17th century; seven panels in height with narrow moulded framing finished by a slender cornice. Similar panelling is contained in the doors and window linings. On the north side of the room is a fluted pilaster with moulded capping to a panelled pedestal. The chimney piece, also original, is of wood and the fireplace opening is flanked by pairs of half round shafts standing on panelled pedestals supporting a shelf with deep sloping sides. Above are three pairs of shafts supporting narrow scrolls and cornice with raised moulded panels between them. The chimney piece is far too large for the room and although of the right date, early 17th century, it probably came from elsewhere. There is a small vestibule which may once have been used as a shared cupboard or wardrobe between this and the room next door. What appear to be the outline of a doorway into this cupboard can be seen in the panelling next to the fireplace.

The panelling, cornice, doors and fireplace of the room over the Rainton Room are similar to those over the Drawing room. Although the ground floor of the south-west extension at least is believed to have been constructed in the early years of the 17th century, 1636, all the internal fittings in the upper room are of the late 18th century or early 19th century date.

Three rooms were added over the housekeeper's room in c1897 for use as a bathroom, WC and a dressing room. The latter has a fireplace containing a 19th century cast iron grate.

Floor boards on the first floor are of wide oak planks screwed into position with the exception of the middle room and the area at the head of the stairs which have narrow, well worn boards which are obviously much older.

Second Floor

'In the Attic, The Accommodation for the Servants are sufficiently numerous' (1773)

It is uncertain what structural alterations were made when most of the rooms on this floor were refitted during the 18th century. There are eight rooms, together with the head of the backstairs and a WC inserted into the narrow space alongside, again no doubt replacing an earlier earth closet. The south-east room appears to be original and has a sloping ceiling formed by the lower part of the roof with an ogee moulding and grotesque masks in the angles. There is a plain architrave at the junction of the ceiling and walls.

All the rooms on the second floor have fireplaces with cast iron surrounds, with the exception of three small bedrooms which occupy most of the east side where conditions in winter must have been rather spartan. However, in the corridor outside is a large unplastered chimney breast which carried smoke and fumes from the bedroom fires below and from the kitchen range; the warmed brickwork of this chimney breast would have provided some ambient heat to this part of the upper floor.

30 Drawing of chimney piece in the middle room on the second floor

31 Plaster mask on the ceiling of the south-east room on the second floor

Basement

'The cellars are roomy and dry, paved with Purbeck and the Wine Vaults substantially arched' (1773)

There are two brick lined vaulted wine cellars with bays for wine racks beneath the Great Hall. Other cellars with stone floors are below the Drawing Room, the Rainton Room and the south-west wing. In the southwest corner is the former boiler room and next door is the coal store with its coal chute beneath the southwest wing. This part of the cellar was later extended beneath the area occupied by the large bay added to the room above in 1897.

Examination of the cellar floor revealed a small, neatly-constructed brick drain which enters the base of one wall and emerges a short distance away in another part of the cellar. Brick-lined gullies connect with this drain and there is a sump in one corner where they eventually terminate. There are two large lead water pipes fastened to the tops of the walls and these cross the cellar at different points to pass through the external walls of the house. One pipe enters the far end of one of the wine cellars, the floor of which is raised, apparently to accommodate one of the drains which runs beneath it. It is possible that one of the two 'wine cellars' was a cold store for food where a low temperature was maintained by the use of ice which would require some form of drainage when the ice melted. A remnant of lath and plaster trapped behind one of the ceiling beams shows that part of the cellar at least had plastered ceilings.

Sanitation

Apart from the indoor privies previously mentioned, there would have been at least one outside privy, tucked away behind a tree or in a shrubbery, in the stable yard or an outhouse, or possibly at the end of a garden path. It would have consisted of a wooden seat built over a cess pit. In Georgian times privies were sometimes disguised as a temple or follies, but this does not appear to have been the case at Forty Hall. In fact, we have no idea what the Jericho or necessary house, as it later became known, looked like or where it was situated. In addition a supply of chamber pots would have been kept in bedside cabinets or in commodes disguised as a stool or chair. Servants would carry the chamber pots down the main staircase at a discreet moment and empty them into the cess pit(s) in the grounds.

It is a matter for conjecture when earth closets were fitted in Forty Hall and although water closets became available in the 18th century they were not fitted as a matter of course. Whatever was in use before the end of the 19th century, one gets the impression that an efficient sanitation system was not installed there until the programme of modernisation was carried out in 1897.

Water Supplies

Another feature almost certainly lacking at Forty Hall until the end of the 19th century was running water. Water was obtained from wells dug for this purpose in the grounds and three wells are known there. In the kitchen garden is a well once used by the gardeners. On the east side of the outer courtyard the brickwork of a well head can be seen which would have supplied water for the washhouse, brewhouse and laundry and probably the slaughterhouse, mentioned in the 18th century sale catalogue and for the kitchen. What appears to be the site of another well, on the south side of the lawn at the rear of the house, is indicated in very dry weather by a circle of grass which remains green long after the rest of the lawn has turned brown. No doubt there are other wells awaiting discovery elsewhere in the grounds.

Bathing was not always a frequent exercise amongst any level of society in the early 17th century when washing of the face and hands and, later on, an all over wash from a bowl in the bedroom, was often the norm. Later still a hip-bath was used, the water for which would have to be carried upstairs by servants and back down again when the bath was emptied. It has already been mentioned that plumbing was almost certainly first installed at Forty Hall at the end of the 19th century. A boiler was fitted in the basement and connected to radiators used to provide central heating as well as hot water to rooms converted for use as bathrooms. Although hip-baths were then abandoned, the marble topped wash stand with its jug and basin and slop pail below probably continued in use for a morning wash with water brought upstairs in copper or brass cans.

Heating & Lighting

Heating at Forty Hall was first provided by open fires fuelled by wood or coal, but the house with its large rooms would have been cold and draughty by the standards of today. More clothing, especially wool, was worn in those days and beds were four poster with curtains which when drawn made a room within a room — no doubt very stuffy but much warmer than outside. A major problem is highlighted by the helpful hints in the 'Young Woman's Companion' of 1765; 'let open the windows of bedchambers and uncover beds to sweeten them; which will be a great help against bugs and fleas. Sponge with a mixture of spirits of wine, spirits of turpentine and campfire'. An 18th century advertisement proclaimed itself as: 'Bug destroyers to Her Majesty'.

Candles provided the only form of lighting for many years. Effective, i.e. smokeless, oil lamps were not produced until c1780 and gas lighting did not became readily available until the 1860's, with electricity following shortly afterwards.

Furniture

In the early 17th century, furniture was very heavy but became lighter by the end of the century. Stools or box chairs provided seating and were made more comfortable by the addition of cushions and later by woven or padded seats. Wooden chests for storage were eventually replaced by chests of drawers, and there were cupboards for storing plate, china and glass. The introduction of mahogany and the ease with which it could be carved influenced subsequent furniture design. Furniture was for the most part placed against walls, and the dado rail was introduced to prevent damage to panelling and other wall coverage. It was not until the Regency period (1811-1820) that armchairs and settees were grouped around fireplaces.

4
The Courtyards

'Double Courts are formed by the exterior Offices; though that consitute the Inner, are large Coach Houses, Stabling, Granary, Barns, Brewhouse, Millhouse, Laundry and other various Buildings, all brick built and in excellent Repair'. (1773)

Inner Courtyard

To the north-west of the house is a courtyard, originally surfaced with gravel, flanked on the south and west sides by 17th century buildings of brick with peg-tile roofs. The eastern side of the courtyard was originally enclosed by a brick wall from the corner of the north-west wing of the house to a point beside the

32 Entrance to the inner courtyard 1932

east gate lodge (SP PLAN). It was re-aligned when an extension was added to the front of the north-east extension some time before the middle of the 19th century. A further alteration was necessary following the construction of the servants hall in 1928 when the wall was rebuilt along a line from the south-east corner of the gate lodge to the north-west corner of the new servants hall (OS 1865, 1936). In c1951 this wall was in turn demolished for most of its length when public conveniences were built there.

Standing on the north side of the courtyard, the gateway has been described as being constructed in the Artisan-Mannerist style of the 1630s (VCH). Brick piers support a large central arch in rusticated brickwork which terminate in pyramidal structures topped with stone balls. In the centre, above the arch, is a curvilinear gable with a triangular pediment. There are smaller arches on either side with embattled work along the top and extending along the adjoining walls. Stone voussoirs are incorporated in the arches and square stone blocks top the imposts. Small brick lodges with hipped and peg-tile roofs, elliptical windows, arched doorways and brick lined floors below present ground level stand within the courtyard on each side of the gateway. A curved approach to the central arch was paved with brick with wide stone edges along which the iron tyred wheels of carriages and other vehicles could travel without causing damage to the surface of the drive when entering or leaving the courtyard. Stone bollards stood at the bases of the gate piers to protect the brickwork from damage by the same vehicles. The gateway was heavily restored in 1967 during work by Firmin and Son of Enfield and at the same time iron gates were hung in the previously open arched entrances.

The ranges of buildings on the south and west were extensively rebuilt with new doors and windows inserted during the 1960s and little now remains of any original features. Fortunately, a detailed survey was made by members of the Royal Commission of Historical Monuments in 1937 and the full hand-written report has survived. This report, together with photographs and drawings in the local history collection and recollections of people who were associated with the house and grounds when it was a private estate or who were involved in the reconstruction work of the 1960s and 1970s, enabled an identification of some, at least, of the purposes for which parts of these buildings were used.

The roofs were of the simplest with tie beams on which rested braces to support the rafters. Both ranges were two-storied, with the upper floors extending into the roof space. The west range, from the gable roof to the point where the roof line drops sharply to the lower level, appeared to have been built first. At the north end there was an original doorway which had been blocked and an extension added. The lower roofed extension contained an ogee moulded frame of a three light window with diagonal bars in the eastern wall. At the northern end was a similar window of two lights in the ground storey and another partly altered above. All were considered to be of early 17th century date and the extension must have been constructed shortly after the completion of the main part of the west range. On the west side of the range were additional and later extensions, but another at the southern end was a two storey wing which may have been original.

The Kitchen

'... and other domestic Offices (of which there are in abundance) are copiously furnished for every Family purpose' (1773).

Within the south range of the courtyard building, at the eastern end, were located the original kitchen and scullery separated by a large fireplace, long since blocked (RCHM) which had a chimney containing four diagonally placed flues. On the opposite, scullery, side were two brick recesses with moulded stone lintels. In the ceiling was a moulded beam with ogee shaped stops which during renovation work in the 1960's was re-positioned at the western end of the wing within the structure of the present banqueting suite. A doorway from the courtyard led to an enclosed internal staircase which gave access to the bedrooms of the butler and footman. Apart from the tie beams the whole of the roof of the south range has been rebuilt, but the way in which the roof abutted on the rafters of the west range suggested that it has been built a little later. It was during the 18th century that the colonnades on the south and east sides of the courtyard were added.

During the alterations carried out in the 1960s, the upper floors, kitchen fireplace and chimney stack were removed and the remaining interiors of all the courtyard buildings were completely rebuilt destroying the surviving 17th century and later features within. The former kitchen and scullery were converted into an exhibition gallery, the stables next door are now a cafeteria and the carriage house in the west range is a banqueting suite. A large stone sink which undoubtedly came from either the original kitchen in the courtyard building or the later kitchen in the middle room, is today in use as a flower container and stands against the north wall of the cottage and stable block flanking the outer courtyard.

There were many changes in use made for the various parts of the courtyard buildings since the description given in the 18th century catalogues, and no doubt before then. Outlines of loops with splayed jambs revealed the positions of windows long since blocked, with new doors and windows fitted elsewhere. When the horse drawn coach gave way to the motor car, the coach room housed a portable petrol driven electric generator and there was also a battery room. The old brewhouse in the lower roofed extension in the west range, with a kiln or oven in the north-west corner with its brick chimney, became a storeroom with a wood store next door. It is not known exactly where the granary, millhouse and laundry described in the 18th century sale catalogue were located. The uses to which the various parts of these buildings were put and the layout of the estate as a whole, as detailed in the sale catalogues, show how self-sufficient a small country house had to be and that a small army of servants would be required to carry out all the duties necessary to ensure the comfort of the family living there.

During excavations by the Enfield Archaeological Society on the north lawn in 1993 an unlined arched brick drain was discovered. Its course was from the direction of the inner courtyard and across the lawn. Within the inner courtyard were a brewhouse and laundry, with a slaughterhouse not far away in the outer courtyard beyond. These places would require the use of considerable amounts of water and the drain was probably used to dispose of waste products. The eventual destination of the drain is not known but it is likely that the contents would be discharged into a distant soakaway.

Outer Courtyard

'Those more remote, are calculated for the Conduct of a Farm, and contain, large Barns, Stables, Cow and Cart Houses, Slaughter House, Sties, &c. &c. &c together with complete Dog Kennel and Rick Yard adjoining' (1773)

Buildings 'calculated for the Conduct of a Farm' at Forty Hall were contained within an enclosure of 17th century date surrounding the outer courtyard. The boundaries of this enclosure consist of: on the east side, a range of buildings now forming the modern banquetting suite which replaced earlier structures demolished or largely rebuilt in the 1960s; the north wall of the kitchen garden; the former warren and the 'lane from Forty Hall to the New River' (SP 1773, SPPLAN). The entrance to the courtyard is opposite the end of the approach road from the lodge.

A long, narrow eight-bayed building, part brick, part timber-framed, occupies most of the north side of the courtyard. The date of construction of this building was recently thrown into doubt when core samples taken from some of the timbers gave a felling date of 1475. An examination of the carpentry joints used in its construction indicates that the timbers concerned are unlikely to represent re-used material brought from elsewhere. If this is correct then that part at least of the wall used as a base for the north side of the building must be much earlier than the rest of the enclosure wall.

Two bays at the eastern end in use as a small cottage by the 1940s were completely rebuilt c1980 for use by the park rangers but it now stands empty. A centrally-placed brick chimney containing three pots with another chimney on the north side date from the time when an earlier cottage had been used by a gardener. In the 1930s the cottage had become so dilapidated that the gardener was moved to another cottage in the grounds of the nearby Dower House. Before that, it was probably used by the stockman of Forty Hall Farm.

Originally a timber-framed structure, the purpose of which is not known, the four central bays were rebuilt in brick and a timber upper floor was installed for use as a hay loft, access to which was by means of a vertical ladder. It is at this time that the building is considered to have come into use as a stable. During the 19th century, the east gable wall was removed and replaced with brick and an outshot added and the two remaining bays also became stables. In the early days of the 20th century, the two bays next to the cottage were converted for use as a mess room for farm staff. The south wall facing the courtyard has been much altered and the present fenestration dates only from the late 19th century or even early 20th century. A large area of Flemish bond in yellow stock brick blocks a former wagon entrance (WITTRICK).

During excavations by the Museum of London Archaeology Service in November 1994, test pits were dug alongside the south wall of the stable block when parts of a cobbled area were exposed. Beneath the cobbles were traces of other surfaces which led to the conclusion that a much earlier building may have stood nearby. On the east side of the gateway part of the courtyard wall has been incorporated into a later brick building with a gabled peg tile roof.

The buildings on the east side of the outer courtyard were demolished or substantially rebuilt during the construction of the banquetting suite during the 1960s. A drawing (F H COLL) shows the gateway in the north wall of the courtyard and the surviving building just described near the entrance with a larger house since demolished just beyond. This last house had lattice windows with banding between the two storeys and a hipped roof and it must have been the original south-west wing referred to in 1937 (RHCM). The section of the garden wall containing the gateway was demolished to make room for an extension of the present banquetting suite. Part of the brickwork of a well-head, previously mentioned, can be found

33 Entrance to the outer courtyard today

34 Entrance to the outer courtyard c1900

beneath bushes near the kitchen door of the banquetting suite.

Whatever buildings stood against the north kitchen garden wall, one of which was a gardner's cottage, have gone, but the cartographic evidence shows that they were not constructed earlier than the first half of the 19th century (c 1865). Viewed from within the courtyard, the brickwork of the garden wall is much

35 Stables in the outer courtyard

36 Main barn dividing the outer courtyard in two

more decorative than from the kitchen garden, and the increase in height by several rows of bricks can be clearly seen from this side.

Most of the central part of the courtyard is occupied by a large timber-framed barn which effectively divides the area in two. It is a part-aisled timber-framed structure of five bays with part brick, part timber-framed gable end walls and is clad in timber weather-boarding with a roof of clay peg tiles bedded in mortar. A detailed examination and the results of excavation inside and around the outside of the structure show that no earlier than the 18th century a barn of three bays with large wide doorways at the front and rear of the central bay began to be constructed. Changes in design were made during its construction when an extra bay was added at either end and the central area, originally intended for threshing, was used for access and distribution. An aisle at the rear was added in the late 19th century and part of the roof reconstructed. The aisle was probably derived from an earlier 'outshot' with a brick floor at a lower level than the wooden floor of the main barn. The wooden floor was eventually overlaid with successive clay floors, which were replaced as they wore out. Excavation also revealed substantial brickwork which may not be directly

37 Building in south-west corner of the outer courtyard from Warren field

related to the existing structure and may even be the remains of an earlier two storey brick building but, it must be emphasised, further work would be necessary to determine this point. The bricks used in these foundations were well-fired, with shallow frogs and are probably contemporary with those used in the construction of Forty Hall. To the east of the barn, more of the cobbled yard was found, the full extent of which has yet to be determined. (MOLAS, WITTRICK).

The area of the outer courtyard behind the barn must have been the rick yard mentioned in the 1773 sale catalogue. Only one small building is shown in this area, part of which could have contained the dog kennel described in the 18th century sale catalogues — corn was a valuable commodity and dogs were often housed in specially built kennels as protection against thieves. This building, in the south-west corner of the outer courtyard, began as a single storey brick building, in mainly English bond, structurally integrated with the enclosure wall and formed part of the original layout of the early 17th century. The high quality of the brickwork is not found elsewhere on the site and is considered unusual in a building of this status. During the late 17th or early 18th century, an upper storey was added with the west gable end in Flemish bond, raised on the enclosure wall. Its purpose is unclear but a large window in the upper floor of the west elevation overlooking the warren may suggest some connection with this activity — possibly a keepers cottage. In later years it became a garden potting shed. The roof is modern and was probably replaced when the building was extended to the east, c1900 (WITTRICK).

Test pits revealed a scatter of brick and mortar rubble representing constructional debris from buildings erected in the rick yard and the area to the west during the early years of 20th century (MOLAS). There was corresponding building activity on the other side of the lane to the north of the outer courtyard, where there were no buildings at all in the 18th century (SP PLAN) but several sprang up there during the 19th century. Many were obviously of an ephemeral nature, put up for a specific purpose; sheds, a saw mill and so on, and they disappeared almost as quickly as they had appeared (OS 1865, 1896, 1914 & 1936).

Many of the alterations made to existing buildings were probably the result of changes in farming methods during the 18th and 19th centuries. Whatever type of farming had been practised earlier, the mention of cow houses, sties and a slaughterhouse in the 18th century sale catalogues shows that cattle and pigs were raised and slaughtered there (SP 1773, 1787). However, a large barn, rick yard and granary referred to in the same catalogues which list various ploughs, harrows and a chaff cutter (SP FEB 1787) reveal that arable farming was once a feature of the Home Farm economy. Perhaps the cessation of arable farming was related to the changes in design and use of the stable block and in particular the large barn. Arable farming was reintroduced during the Second World War. Cattle, in the form of a dairy herd, were still being kept on the Home Farm, together with a few sheep, pigs and chickens, during the 1920s and 1930s. In the 1950s it was entirely given over to sheep, but, following proposals to turn the area occupied by the derelict farm buildings and the surrounding fields into an equestrian centre, with a museum devoted to the history of the working horse, all the sheep and farm machinery were sold in the early part of 1996.

5
The Grounds

Front Lawn & Lake

Contained within the curve of the carriage drive at the front of the house, a semi-circular lawn slopes towards the edge of a nearby lake. In 1993 the retaining wall of the lake was collapsing and the Enfield Borough Council proposed to lower the level of the lawn and thus avoid the use of a retaining wall altogether. Two machine-dug trenches to find out what lay beneath the surface of the lawn revealed the base of a low brick wall and a brick vaulted drain. Part of a wine bottle c1740 was recovered from one of the trenches (SOC NEWS a). At the request of the London Borough of Enfield, excavations by the Enfield Archaeological Society were carried out later in the same year; a description of the brick drain has already been given. The brickwork of the wall crosses the middle of the lawn from east to west and was in two sections, each terminating just before the centre in a larger square of brickwork, perhaps as bases on which

38 Excavations on the north lawn 1993

39 Excavated 17th century drain on the north lawn 1993

to stand vases, statues or some other form of garden ornament. The gap in the centre was probably occupied by a shallow flight of steps giving access from one level to another of a terraced garden, a feature of Jacobean gardens. The bricks were similar to those used in the construction of the house and suggests an early 17th century date for this part of the garden layout. The terraces themselves may have been occupied by parterres; box and other shrubs set in regular patterns with coloured earth arranged between them; although they could equally well have been grassed surfaces bisected with gravel paths.

There is no record to tell us when the terraces were levelled or why this was done. Apart from changes in fashion, one reason could have been the tendency for the lawn with its high water table to flood very easily. A situation no doubt exacerbated by the transverse brickwork along the edge of the terrace and the brick drain. In any event, a later field drain consisting of short lengths of clay pipes each with a flat base set end to end cut through the brickwork and the remains of the demolished brick drain and continued to the edge of the lake. Two other drains are known to have crossed the lawn; one from the north-east corner of the house to an outlet in the retaining wall at the edge of the lake, and can be seen in the 19th century photograph of the house and lake (P 1984), and the other from the north-west corner of the house to an outlet which can still be seen in the retaining wall of the lake.

On the edge of the lawn, close to the main entrance to the house are two stone lions. One came from Broomfield following the disastrous fire there in 1984 but the other, now heavily eroded, has been there for some considerable time. The late 19th century photograph in the local collection (P 1894) shows the lion, and an earlier 1823 pen and ink drawing (GENTS MAG e) appears to show the same object. No attempt has been made to analyse the material from which they were made but it could be Coade stone; an artificial ceramic resembling limestone produced by Mrs Eleanor Coade at her kilns in Lambeth from 1769. A wide variety of decorative objects were made from this material and the kilns remained in production until 1843.

At the lower end of the lawn is an irregularly-shaped artificial lake, far too informal in outline to be original. If water had been introduced as an ornamental feature here in the early 17th century it is more likely to have been in the form of a square pond or even a water parterre. Equally likely is that the line of terraced parterres from the front of the house continued across the later site of the lake to the boundary of the grounds at that time, which today is represented by the lower approach road.

In fact, the insertion of a water feature may well have been carried out after the adjoining land containing the remnants of Elsyng Palace had been incorporated into the grounds of Forty Hall during the second half of the 17th century. By this date it had become traditional to occupy land in front of the house with parterres, often with a water feature, either a water parterre or a canal, and in the background a park

40 Part of the brickwork of a retaining wall for a garden terrace found during excavations on the north lawn 1993

displaying ornamental plantings such as the avenue of trees at Forty Hall.

When the lake was dug, or perhaps re-cut from an existing water feature during the 18th century, the upcast was used to create a mound, now covered with trees, on the west side of the lake. The fact that the soil was deliberately placed there in that way suggests that it was intended as a garden mount, popular from Tudor times to the 18th century, which would have provided an elevated view from within an arbour or gazebo. In this case, the mount would not need to be very high in order to obtain a view across the adjoining park.

On the east side of the mount are the graves of four dogs, each with an inscribed headstone.

Little	Tinker Bowles	Caesar	Cinder
Susie	The dearest of dogs	a puppy	died June 13th 1910
harmless	11 years old	1934	aged 12 years
victim of a	1934		the best of dogs
bloodthirsty act			most faithful friend
1937			

Little Susie was Lady Bowles' dog and the 'bloodthirsty act' was the accidental shooting of the animal by the gamekeeper, Mr Miles, who was looking for a fox at the time. The inscription was composed by the butler of the household who did not like Mr Miles. (SMITH)

On the north side of the lake is the approach road to the outer courtyard. A late 18th century painting (DAYES) and the Breton plan (BRETON) shows a fence standing between the edge of the lake and the road. The island in the centre of the lake is of relatively recent construction, c1970s, and was built to provide a refuge for water fowl.

Pleasure Grounds

'In the PLEASURE GROUND (an elegant Green House) the lawn bordered by a rich Plantation of Shrubs and Evergreens, that conceal and adorn circuitous walks, that gradually slope to the Lodge at the Approach' (1773)

41 Garden mount, now overgrown with trees

42 View from second floor windows of the house showing north lawn, lake and avenue of trees beyond

A brick retaining wall supports a wide terrace now paved with flagstones laid c1951 to replace the former gravel surface along the east side of the house. Modern materials have been used to rebuild steps from the terrace to the ground below opposite the east porch and further along a more ornamental stone serves the same purpose. Beyond, at a lower level, the sloping wall continues and holds in place the edge of the raised lawn. For the whole of its length the wall is made of good quality bricks, each with a frog with the maker's initials inside — unfortunately, the few exposed bricks are too heavily eroded to read the initials. The southern edge of the lawn is a grassed terrace. The cartographic evidence shows several trees standing in the area of the lawn during the mid-19th century (OS 1865) but by the end of the century they had gone (OS 1896), which together with the evidence of the type of brick used for the retaining wall indicated that the lawn in its present form was not laid until well into the second half of the 19th century.

The stone paved terrace, decorated with urns standing on plinths — some of which were replaced during the 1950s — extends along the rear of the house. In the centre is an area paved with flag stones with diamond shaped insets — the same design used in the floor of the east porch — which leads to a flight of steps descending to the lawn. A photograph taken in 1894 shows that the terrace was not constructed until the end of the 19th century and must be a part of the work carried out by Henry Ferryman Bowles (P 1894).

Against the wall of the house next to the south porch is a large magnolia. Soon after the purchase of the estate by the Enfield council, a lead label inscribed 'Magnolia Grandiflora planted in 1852' was found fastened to the back wall of the house (GUIDE). Further along, the paved area widens and is laid at two levels and there are two more steps leading up to a larger paved area in front of the orangery which continues to the wall of the kitchen garden. Until c1951 only a small part of the ground in front of the orangery was paved, the rest formed part of the surrounding shrubbery.

Around the perimeter of the pleasure ground on the east side and at the rear of the house is a belt of trees and shrubs which screen the grounds from Forty Hill and was extended to hide the east wall of the kitchen garden. Within the trees, which contain many interesting and often exotic varieties — note the examples of the palm family near the house — is a circuitous path from the terrace at the rear of the house to a point on the carriage drive near the entrance lodge. This arrangement is reminiscent of the belt-walks developed during the 18th century where irregularly planted trees with a walk, sometimes a drive, kept the grounds very private by excluding external views. On the east side of the belt-walk the path emerged from the trees for a short distance to allow members of the family and their guests taking a stroll to look across the grounds (SP PLAN). Later on, more trees were planted there to create a narrow vista through which walkers would suddenly be provided with a view focused on the east elevation of the house (OS 1865). The vista was still there in the early years of 20th century but, after the re-building of the lodge in 1903, it was reduced to a small glade (OS 1913), part of which can still be seen. The line of the former view was later firmly blocked by a tennis court (OS 1936) and later still, c1940s, a small wooden summer house stood nearby but this together with the tennis court have since, c1951, been removed.

Within the area enclosed by the belt-walk the ground had previously been landscaped to form a large sloping grassed terrace in a fashion common in this country in the 17th century and there is evidence of more terracing along the edge of the grounds in Forty Hill which continues beyond the small entrance gate inserted c1951. The terrace here also marks the curve of the drive which although it still leads to the Dower House was after 1896 reduced in width. At the same time a pond which stood nearby (SP PLAN) was filled-in (OS 1865, 1896). The south wall of the pleasure grounds contains an entrance fitted with a wrought iron gate through which access was gained to the drive leading to the Dower House.

The only mention of garden layout so far discovered which could possibly refer to Forty Hall is in a note amongst the Gough papers in the Bodleian Library. Unfortunately, part of the wording has been obscured by the binding of the folder in which it is contained, but in the visible remainder there are references to 'the front' (forecourt?), 'cut yews', 'holly hedge', 'a grove of oaks', 'cultivated/planted by Leeson'. Elsewhere in the Gough papers is a reference to 'a house opposite Mr Breton's gate belonging to Maize formerly Leeson.' Was Leeson therefore the manager of the Forty Hall estate during the 18th century?

A cedar of Lebanon mentioned in the 1773 and 1787 sale catalogues is still standing on the lawn on the east side of the house. These trees were introduced into this country in the 17th century when they became very popular and there were few country houses which did not have at least one planted in their grounds. In 1850 William Keane refers to '… some handsome Cedars of Lebanon' at Forty Hall but he had mistakenly identified another cedar tree of a different kind which stood nearby (KEANE). This second cedar survived until a few years ago when it was blown down in a gale.

A large rhododendron near the house featured in a pen and ink drawing published in 1823 (GENTS MAG E). Rhododendrons were first introduced into this country from America in the mid-18th century and a hundred years later other varieties were brought back from the Orient. However, the rhododendrons in the grounds of Forty Hall were almost certainly all hybrids of garden origin (HERBARIUM).

The first reference to a greenhouse at Forty Hall is made at the end of the 17th century; 'Mr Raynton's garden at Enfield is observable for nothing but his greenhouse, which he has had for many years. His orange, lemon and myrtle trees are as full and furnished as any in cases' (GIBSON). These early greenhouses contained very little glass in their construction and were 'houses' into which were placed 'greens', plants in tubs and pots, for protection from the cold during winter months. During the summer months, they were probably used to outline a formal walk; perhaps in the sheltered southerly aspect at the rear of the house. If oranges, introduced from France in 1562, were included the building in which they were kept became known as an orangery. Orange and lemon trees continued to be grown at Forty Hall until 1786 when 49 such trees were put up for sale after the death of Eliab Breton in the previous year (SP 1786). William Keane describes the greenhouse as being 40 feet long and situated between the cedar trees and the kitchen garden (KEANE), and its location is shown on the 1773 sale plan as standing against the south gable of the west range of courtyard buildings in the angle formed by the nearby kitchen garden wall. The only direct reference to it as an 'orangery' is in 1911; 'ÖÖan orangery has been fitted up by Colonel H F Bowles J P as an aquarium for the presentation of rare fish and specimens of marine biology' (WHITAKER). The original building has been extensively modified and is now part of the adjoining banqueting suite. An odd feature in its construction is that although the sides are parallel to one another they are not at right angles to the front wall.

Walled Kitchen Garden

> 'The kitchen Garden adjoins, is walled round and planted with Fruit Trees, and capable of producing vegetables in vast profusion.' (1773)

Kitchen gardens, usually walled, were common in this country from the 17th century to the 19th and a walled kitchen garden two acres in extent and contemporary with the house stands south-west of Forty Hall. It was conveniently placed immediately behind the outer courtyard for the transfer of manure from the stables. The walls are about eight feet in height and at first glance appear to be rectangular in plan but closer study reveals that no two sides are of equal length. The north wall is aligned on the same axis as the house but none of the other garden walls are at right angles to it.

There are two 17th century references to a walled garden at Forty Hall:

> ... the orchard garden and close adjoining inclosed with a Bricke Wall in the occupation of the said Nicholas Raynton Esq. ... (R 1656)

> He has a myrtle cut in the shape of a chair, that is at least six feet high from the base, but the lower part is bare of leaves. The rest of the garden is very ordinary, and on the outside of his garden he has a warren, which makes the ground about his seat lie rudely and sometimes the coneys work under the wall into his garden. (GIBSON)

At the northern end of the garden on the east side there is a short length of wall, together with another wall about 8 feet long at right angles to it. It is not known when the rest of the wall was demolished. A few feet of wall was later rebuilt using blocks of overfired bricks which are fused together. The surface of the garden slopes from west to east and foundations seen as a parch mark during dry weather may be those of a low retaining wall, just sufficiently high to keep the garden soil in place and prevent it from encroaching on the tree-lined walk between it and the outer garden wall, now represented by a hedge.

Evidence of repairs and re-building can be seen in the surviving walls but apart from the north wall no recognisable bond can be seen in the brickwork. In the north wall the bricks are laid in English bond except for the top seven courses, laid in irregular fashion at a later date.

Kitchen gardens usually had three entrances (STUART) and Forty Hall conformed, more or less, to this arrangement. There is a small entrance in the east wall at the north-east corner for use of the family, another was in the north wall from the outer courtyard but this disappeared when an extension to existing buildings was added in the 1960s. The former entrance in the south wall has already been mentioned. Next to it, in the west wall, is another entrance leading into Warren Field, but this is of relatively recent construction. The last entrance to be made was in the north-west corner of the garden which became necessary when more farm build-

43 Basil, head gardener, standing at the north end of the kitchen garden, 1894

ings were erected some time before the middle of the 19th century.

Some internal details can be seen on the 1773 sale plan which shows trees around the inside of the south and west walls which were also bordered by paths. There were more trees in the centre and the rest of the enclosed area was divided into plots or 'quarters' for growing vegetables. A small building is shown in the south-east corner of the garden, perhaps used to store garden tools, as its successor does today. The later Breton plan also gives some details of the interior of the walled garden and shows the outline of a large square-shaped plot, divided in two by a path with an apsidal shaped feature in the centre of the south side, occupying the top third of the garden. But it is the first edition of the Ordnance Survey 25 inch plan published in 1866 that shows the first really detailed layout of the garden with path-lined borders along the insides if the walls with other paths again dividing the ground into 'quarters', thus enabling the gardeners to carry out an organised programme of vegetable growing. A number of fruit trees stand in the eastern half of the garden and there would be others espaliered against the walls. There was also the double line of what could be more fruit trees between the two walls on the east side of the garden. A centrally placed greenhouse with a forecourt contained a well and another greenhouse stood in the north-west corner. One of the greenhouses would undoubtedly have been a vinery, perhaps both, in order to provide early and late crops of grapes, as well as a range of other fruits, melons, peaches, figs and so on, for the household.

Subsequent editions of the Ordnance Survey 25 inch plans never again gave such minute details as the first edition but although ground divisions are lacking, structures such as greenhouses continue to be shown. We can see that by the end of the 19th century another greenhouse had been placed next to the one in the north-west corner, and another next to the one in the centre of the garden. By the 1930s the three greenhouses in the south-west corner of the garden had been removed, leaving only the two in the centre. The tree-lined walk between the parallel east walls and the small building in the south-west corner were still there in the mid-1930s (OS 1936).

The plots or 'quarters' within the garden were lined with box, most of which was grubbed-up in the 1950s, apart from one length which survives near the north wall. The two remaining greenhouses survived until the 1950s when they and most of the other features were also removed and the interior of the garden was then grassed. Wall borders and circular beds in the grassed area were created and at first were planted with roses but since replaced with shrubs.

However, apart from the length of box hedging near the north wall, there is a fig tree close to the entrance in the west wall and a wisteria of some age in the opposite corner by the east gateway. There is also a square-shaped well-head, the stonework of which bears a circular wreath enclosing a blank shield carved on opposing sides. Shorn of its windlass, it has been sealed by a block of stone. Nearby was a large brick-built water tank, about 15 feet by 10 feet in area with a parapet about 2 feet high. It was supplied with water from a standpipe and this structure made it much easier and quicker for gardeners to obtain water than by using the well. A mulberry tree also survived. It stood in the central position at the north end of the garden but was blown down during the hurricane of 1987. Drainage was improved by the insertion of field drains at some time during the 19th century and the clay pipes of one such drain can be seen protruding from the surface of the gravel path near the east entrance to the garden.

The rows of trees planted in orderly fashion outside the west wall of the garden (OS 1866) may have been the successors to the 'orchard garden' referred to in the mid-17th century (R 1656), originally inside the garden and later re-planted outside. By the end of the 19th century the trees had been enclosed (OS 1896) and during the early years of this century trees had been planted all along the outside of the west wall and firmly enclosed within an irregularly-shaped fence or hedge. Twenty years later this boundary had been straightened and ran parallel to the garden wall, with the northern end of the enclosed area occupied by three large greenhouses and two smaller ones; today only the concrete bases remain.

44 Well-head in the kitchen garden

Rabbit Warren

On the west side of the kitchen garden is a field known at the end of the 18th century as The Warren (SP 1773), part of which contained a rabbit warren which was there in the 17th century and may have been established even earlier for the benefit of the household of Elsyng palace where there was a warrener from the early 16th century at least (PALACES b). The conveyance of Worcesters manor from the Earl of Salisbury to Nicholas Rainton dated 4th July 1616 refers to '... warrens within the manor ...' but does not give any locations (W 1616). More information is given in a document drawn-up in the mid 17th century listing all the lands and tenements in Enfield belonging to Sir Nicholas Rainton:

> One tenement adjoining the said Greate House called Enfield House (Elsyng) in the Occupacon of Thomas Goodyeare, Gentleman
> item. One parcel of Ground lyeing near unto the said messuage or Tenement called the Warren & is a warren for Rabbittes being pasteur Grounde. (R 1656)

This must refer to the original warren of Elsyng, for which a more detailed location is given a few years later:

> Mr Raynton's garden at Enfield ... and on the outside of his garden he has a warren, which makes the ground about his seat lie rudely and sometimes the coneys work under the wall into the garden. (GIBSON)

It is not known when the warren was abandoned but it is safe to assume that Nicholas Rainton eventually resolved the problem by removing the burrowing coneys. In 1911, Colonel Bowles built a fence round Warren field in which he kept deer (WHITAKER) but they were no longer there in c1924.

The Park

> THE PARK is an extensive Tract (surrounded with good Oak Paling) the Land luxuriant, the Trees maturely grown, and finely disposed. To augment the natural beauties of the Vale in Front of the House, a magnificent Lake may be easily formed, the running Brook and Successive Ponds (full of Carp and Tench) uniting to facilitate that noble Plan. (1773)

When Nicholas Rainton purchased the Manor of Worcesters in 1616 the sale did not include Elsyng, the ownership of which had been retained by the Crown when the manor was sold in 1602. Although becoming more and more dilapidated with some parts of the buildings demolished, the remainder continued in occupation and there was even some repair work carried out from time to time. Nicholas Rainton died in 1646 and it was his great-nephew who, by c1656, had acquired the adjoining land which contained the surviving buildings of Elsyng palace.

> One very antient Greate house called Endfield house with the Court yardes Gardens Orchards and Courtyard with ye field adjoining called the Walks ... (R 1656).

This was only a very small part of the lands of the former Royal palace which stood near Maidens brook opposite Forty Hall and extended eastwards towards Maidens Bridge, where irregularities in the surface of the ground can be seen. The surviving buildings remained in occupation until c1656 after which they were demolished and the site levelled and landscaped as part of the grounds of Forty Hall. The high ground on the south side of the farm approach road probably represents the northern boundary of the property described in the 17th century document. Apart from providing evidence of underlying buildings the disturbed ground must also represent the outlines of garden features associated with the palace. There is evidence of terracing in the Great Field where it slopes down to Maidens brook, but without carrying out a resistivity survey and even some excavation it is impossible to define these features more clearly or to make any guess as to their purpose and date. An entrance at the south-west corner of the Great Field has a broad stone lintel and on one side an open metal gate pillar with ornamental ironwork on top. Unfortunately, its fellow on the other side of the gateway has disappeared. The 1773 sale plan shows three square ponds in the Great Field which from their appearance must be artificial.

A major feature at Forty Hall is the double avenue of lime trees which extends across the Great Field in front of the house to Maidens brook, and at one time beyond, and must have been planted after the land was acquired by Nicholas Rainton in c1656. At the bottom of the avenue the ground on the south side of the stream was excavated and flooded to create a wide but shallow expanse of water between the trees, which from a distance gave the impression of a broad river flowing through the grounds. It was the use of water in this kind of contrived situation that gave rise to the story that Andre le Notre, the designer of Versailles, was responsible for the landscaping and layout of the grounds at Forty Hall but although he is traditionally associated with gardens at Greenwich and others in Bedfordshire and Northamptonshire, he never came to this country and any influence he exerted at these places would have been by correspondence or through his imitators. Whitaker appears to have been responsible for starting the story that he was involved with the layout of the grounds at Forty Hall (WHITAKER). The avenue of trees continued from the other side of Maidens brook to the northern boundary of the grounds defined by the old course of the New River.

The archaeological evidence suggests that in order to provide a sufficient volume of water to fill the excavated area between the trees a weir was constructed on the east side of the avenue of trees. By the mid-19th century it had become silted up (OS 1865) and by the 1930s was no longer marked on Ordnance Survey plans. Although obscured by undergrowth, the outline of the feature can still be traced on the ground. The original weir appears to have been replaced by a bridge with brick abutments and the bed of the stream between them paved with brick in c1895 when members of the Bowles family lived at Myddleton House and at Forty Hall.

The planting of a double row of trees on each side of the avenue enabled replacements to be made, should only one or two trees die or be blown down, without having a noticeable effect on the symmetry of the avenue as a whole. However, this would not work in situations such as the hurricane of 1987 when very many of the trees were uprooted. The avenue has since been replanted thanks to the generosity of the Royal Society for the Protection of Birds.

The earliest representation of the grounds in cartographic form was by John Rocque but his map of Middlesex published in 1754 is too small in scale to give much detail. Nevertheless, it does show the avenue of trees beyond Maidens brook, only a small part of which was still there in 1865 and it had disappeared completely before the end of the century (OS 1865, 1896).

> The Canals are fortunately placed for Embellishments, and form Cascades that rush impetuous. The New River's winding Stream begirts the Hills, and overspreads their Acclivities with unfading Verdure. (1773)

The author of the 18th century sale catalogue gave full rein to his imagination as can be seen by this example of hyperbole. Nevertheless, there is the New River and the construction of weirs along Maidens brook would have provided some interesting water features in the form of cascades. The remains of three weirs can be seen at various points along the banks of the stream. One, believed to have been constructed to flood the excavated area at the bottom of the avenue of trees, has already been mentioned. There was another downstream just to the west of Maidens Bridge and another was situated further upstream beyond the lake. The dates of construction of the original weirs are not known but they all appear on the 18th century estate plans and, using the brickwork as a guide, they were all rebuilt c1897.

A large lake about 350 yards long is contained within a stretch of woodland beside Maidens brook just to the west of the site of Elsyng. On the few occasions it has been mentioned it has been described, briefly, as a fish pond, which by implication was associated with Elsyng. A long narrow channel, parallel to Maidens brook for a considerable distance, connects the lake to the stream and keeps the lake supplied with water. The reason for such a long feeder channel was the necessity to tap the stream at a higher level to ensure sufficient flow of water into the lake. However, the remains of brickwork of another weir constructed by earlier engineers show the level of the stream would have been raised to a sufficient height to enable a natural flow of water to enter the lake by means of a transverse channel. Details of this modest but apparently successful piece of engineering is depicted on maps from the late 18th century onwards (SP PLAN, BRETON, OS 1865, 1896, 1913 and 1936).

The 1773 sale plan for Forty Hall shows a square-shaped pond at the east end of the lake connected by a short channel to Maidens brook, and there appears to be another channel between the pond and the lake. Such arrangements would be the minimum requirements for draining, cleaning and generally maintaining a fish pond, within which there were often internal divisions to separate different types of fish. Halfway along the south side of the lake is a detached rectangular pond but without excavation it is impossible to say if it was connected to the lake as part of fish management or if it served an entirely different purpose.

The lake no doubt did have its origin as a medieval fishpond or ponds, probably enlarged during the extensive alterations made when Elsyng became a Royal residence and further alteration and re-styling to make it a decorative feature took place in later times, perhaps when the avenue of trees was planted and other landscaping carried out during the second half of the 17th century. There are four islands in the lake shown on the 1773 sale plan; a large central island with smaller ones at each end and, in the north-east corner, a narrow channel was dug to create the fourth island, which from its appearance suggests a moated water garden. All these islands appear on subsequent plans with the exception of the one to the west of the central island. By the end of the 18th century over half the area around the lake had been planted with trees and since then further planting and natural growth has completely enclosed the lake. Evidence of subsequent landscaping comes in the form of rhododendron bushes which line the

45 Looking south along the avenue of trees in the park

46 View across the lower lake

gravel paths in the wooded area; they are so prolific that it would come as no surprise to learn that some paths had been known as 'rhododendron walks'.

In 1981 the Enfield Borough Council began clearing the silt which had accumulated to a depth of three feet on the bed of the lake and, at the same time, the feeder stream was recut and extended along its new line. Members of the Enfield Archaeological Society kept watch while the work was in progress as a result of which they were able to examine a square-shaped brick feature uncovered at the western end of the lake. It was described as having sides 12 feet in length and set firmly in the bed of the lake. There were six courses of brick in its height and each side was four courses of brick wide; the two outer rows were of good quality brick while the two inner rows were made up of fragments. All the bricks were similar to those used to build Forty Hall. No attempt was made to remove the silt within this feature and it remains in situ on the bed of the re-filled lake. This must be the base of the island at the west end of the lake shown on the 1773 sale plan. Two suggestions regarding its purpose were made at the time of discovery; that it was the base for a summerhouse, or the walls were intended to contain the roots of water lilies or similar plants (SOCIETY NEWS b). There is also the possibility that it could have been the base of a fishing temple.

At the eastern end of the lake, on the south bank, a small but substantial brick-built structure was excavated in 1992 by members of the Enfield Archaeological Society. It had been inserted into the bank of the lake with an open side facing the lake and the rear wall about nine metres from the waters edge. Internally it measured 2.5 metres long by 1.60 metres wide and was about 2 metres deep. The walls on the east and west sides had once supported a vaulted brick roof at about the present ground level. To take the thrust of the roof, two brick buttresses had been added to the west wall and two others probably existed against the damaged east wall. The vaulted roof was known to be complete when dredging of the lake began in 1981, but today only the springers remain. Examination showed that it had been constructed of hand-made bricks without frogs, laid in irregular form of English bond, set in lime mortar with later repair work in Portland cement. The bricks appear to be only slightly later in date than those used in the construction of Forty Hall. It was at first thought to be the chamber of an ice-house, but it was soon discovered that the walls extended well below the surface of the nearby lake and in consequence any ice stored there would be contaminated and would also melt very quickly. In fact, family tradition has it that this was the site of a boathouse, with perhaps a wooden superstructure standing above the brick chamber.

However, most large houses had an ice-house in which large quantities of ice, collected from a nearby lake, were stored and taken as required to be used in storing and preparation of food within the house. It would be surprising if the remains of such a structure were not awaiting discovery elsewhere on the estate.

Alongside the courtyards of Forty Hall there begins 'the lane from Forty Hall down to the New River' (SP 1773). This lane is believed to follow part of the southern boundary of the deer park of Elsyng Palace (SYKES). Linked to the lane are 'The Walks and Double Hedges' (SP 1773 & 1787 lot one). Past a pond on the north side of the lane and just beyond the warren is a belt of trees containing a path or walk leading to Maidens brook. This walk curves round the eastern end of a square-shaped pond where, until the 1950s, there stood a well-built summerhouse, with gabled roof, sash windows and wood floors. A building had stood on this site since at least the 1770s (SP PLAN). The last summerhouse on the site was demolished by Enfield Council during the 1950s. The pond is still there and the outline of the small glade can be traced but all that remains to mark the site of the summerhouse are a few fragments of brick and peg-tile and one or two blocks of stone.

Further along the lane, which has since been truncated long before it reaches the New River, were two more raised walks contained between double hedges. One led northwards to Maidens brook, alongside which it ran before joining the northern end of the first lane described, where a small building, possibly another summerhouse, stood from the middle of the 18th century at least until some time in the second half of the 19th century. The other walk went south to the New River which it followed westwards before turning north for a short distance, where it had been planted on both sides with trees, before it rejoined the lane. At the junction of these two walks with the lane there was a seat from the mid-1920s until c1951 which appears to have been the only surviving part of yet another summerhouse as suggested by brickwork still in situ and a surrounding scatter of peg-tiles from the roof. The raised paths were laid on top of quite substantial banks with side ditches on either side from which the earth to build the banks was obtained. All are now heavily overgrown and the former walks are virtually impenetrable. They remind one of William Lawson's advice in the 17th century concerning the enclosure of gardens by means of a double ditch with the excavated soil being used to make a raised walk between them (LAWSON).

Towards the end of the 19th century, another walk between two hedges but without any earthwork, known in later years as the Damson Walk, was constructed between Warren Field and Long Field and was obviously intended to connect a walk from Gough Park alongside the New River with other walks around Forty Hall (OS 1896, 1913). It must have been very pleasant to walk along the raised paths between the fields, resting occasionally in the strategically placed summerhouses.

47 Bridge abutments and site of earlier weir in Maidens Brook at north end of the avenue of trees

48 Brick foundations of boathouse on edge of lower lake after excavation 1992

Appendices

Appendix One — Arms Displayed in the First Floor Landing Windows
The large window inserted in 1887 on the first floor landing of the main staircase is divided into four sections which contain arms of the Bowles and other families linked to them by marriage or by tradition. They are described in order from left to right. Identification of the arms was made by Robert Noel, Bluemantle Pursuivant of the College of Arms. Supplementary information was added by the author.

49 Arms in first floor landing windows (see also rear cover)

Frame One
The Arms of Garnault of Picardy. They have not been registered in official English armory but this is not surprising since, reasonably enough, Englishmen could not recognise the necessity for re-registering the family arms of distinguished French immigrants — France was after all (except for brief intervals) a monarchy just like England. In *Burke's General Armory* the arms of Garnault are blazoned as follows; Per pale or and azure barry of six and a chief charged with a pale and it cantons divided per bend dexter and sinister respectively all counterchanged overall an escutcheon argent. Anne Garnault married Henry Carington Bowles in 1799 which accounts for the arms of the Garnault family being depicted in the window.

The crest displayed above the arms is the coronet of a viscount; a circlet of gold set with sixteen silver balls, pearls in heraldry, nine of which being seen in representation. The significance of its appearance in the window is not known.

Frame Two
The arms and crest granted to Henry Carington Bowles of Myddleton House, Enfield in 1796. Per pale indented gules and azure, three cups, two and one argent, in each a boar's head erect or, for crest, on a wreath of the colours, a demi boar erect erminois, the sinister shoulder pierced with and arrow argent. The motto; '*ut tibi sic alteri*' (as I do to thee, I do to others).

Frame Three
The arms azure, a chevron mounted between three owls argent on a chief or, a bee proper with a crest on

a mount vert an owl rising proper on the breast a bee as in the arms, were granted to Carington Bowles, of the parish of St Gregory in the City of London, merchant, who represented to the deputy Earl Marshal that he was unable to ascertain his descent from any family of Bowles entered in the College of Arms, and was desirous of using Armorial Ensigns; this grant was made to him under the hands and seals of Garter and Clarenceux, Kings of Arms, on 1 January 1782. The motto provided was: '*ut tibi sic alteri*'. The said Carington Bowles did not record a pedigree providing either his ancestors or his descendants. This is not to be wondered at since the very cause of the petitioning for a grant in the first place was the discovery that he was unable to relate himself to any family of Bowles then on record in the College.

The arms and crest do not feature in either *Burke's General Armory* or *Fairbairn's Crests*, that would be a matter of no consequence except that appearances in BGA and Fairbairn as well as Fox-Davies' Armorial Families testify to the continued vitality and even existence of the old armigerous lines; and consequently the omission of these arms and crest in these volumes is an indication of the likelihood (no more than that) that the line of Carington Bowles had failed in the male line.

The motive for putting the arms of Carington Bowles into the stained glass windows can only be guessed at; it may well have been that Carington Bowles or one of his descendants or near relatives was acquainted with the family, between which parties there had always been an assumption or belief of kinship, vide the name of Carington held in common; the researches that Carington Bowles then undertook in the College of Arms showed in fact that no kinship was demonstrable, but this by itself did not mean that the acquaintanceship or friendship was at an end. The main family might even have helped Bowles with the design of his arms — they may have said to him 'every Bowles known to heraldry so far has had bowls or cups with boar's head — for your own arms why not branch out and have a pun on bowls consisting of a bee and owls'. The family of the bee and owls must somehow have remained in contact with the main family and eventually the arms were immortalised in stained glass.

On the other hand, the reason for the inclusion of the Carington Bowles arms of bee and owls may have been merely that the family decided and thought that it was such a quaint and delightful piece of work.

Frame Four
The motto '*aequm servare mentem*' (to preserve a steady mind) is provided with the arms and crest granted on 6 November 1829 to John Treacher of Stamford Hill in the parish of St John, Hackney in the County of Middlesex, Gentleman, the blazon being; per chevron gules and azure on a chevron between three boar's heads couped argent a cross flory between two grasshoppers respecting each other vert with a crest a boar's head cooped armed or in the mouth a dragon's sinister wing argent.

Edward Treacher married Anne Sarah Bowles, daughter of Henry Carington Bowles, in 1823. The eldest surviving son, also Henry Carington, assumed the surname Bowles by Royal Licence in 1852.

In 1913, Wilma Mary Garnault Bowles, daughter of Henry Ferryman Bowles, married Eustace Parker and he in turn assumed the surname of Bowles by Royal Licence in 1920. The Parker arms, not displayed at Forty Hall, are: gules, a chevron between three leopard's faces or. For crest a leopard head affrontee, erased at the neck or ducally gorged gules. The motto: '*sapere audi*' (dare to be wise).

Appendix Two — The King Arthur Cross

In 1191, the monks of Glastonbury claimed to have found the grave of King Arthur and Queen Guinevere. A shrine to contain their bones was eventually built inside the abbey and remained there until it was destroyed in 1553 during the Reformation. On top of Arthur's coffin an inscribed lead cross was said to have rested. Among those who saw the cross was John Leland who in 1542 gave details of its size and description, and it was illustrated for the first time in the sixth edition of Camden's *Britannia* published in 1607. The fate of the cross is not known although it is said to have been seen in Wells in the 18th century, after which it finally disappeared.

An inscribed lead cross, alleged to be the same one found at Glastonbury, was reported as being recovered from the bed of the lake near Maidens brook in the grounds of Forty Hall during dredging operation there in 1981. The finder, Derek Mahoney, took the cross to the British Museum and allowed the student on duty there to photograph it but he refused her request to leave it for further examination. In fact, apart from this one occasion, Derek Mahoney's cross was never seen again.

Because the lake is part of the public open space owned by the London Borough of Enfield, the Council took Derek Mahoney to court in an attempt to recover the cross. He refused and was then sentenced to two years imprisonment for contempt, although he was released after serving only about half the sentence. The whole episode became a minor cause celebre and the cross was the subject of radio and television programmes and details were published in the national press and local papers (ADVERTISER, SOCIETY NEWS c, TIMES b).

Like the original discovery in 1191, the events of 1981 were part of a clever hoax. There is little doubt that Derek Mahoney had manufactured a copy of the cross and made up the story about his finding it in order to obtain publicity for his legal battle with a firm of solicitors and an estate agent concerning the sale of a house. He had been a lead pattern maker working for a well-known local firm of toy-makers who produced detailed lead models of cars. He had also been for some years a member of the Enfield Archaeological Society and had given considerable help on occasions with Carbon-14 dating and in taking x-rays of iron objects from excavations carried out by the Society.

50 The leaden plate in the form of a Cross found in King Arthur's grave at Glastonbury Abbey in the reign of King Henry II. The inscription reads: Hic jacet sepultus inclytus Rex Arthurus in Insula Avalonia ('Here lies interred in the Isle of Avalon the renowned King Arthur')

However, only limited technical expertise was required as the author also carried out some experiments and was able to prove that it is not difficult to cast a copy of the cross in question.

A degree of verisimilitude was added to the story of the local discovery by the fact that the antiquarian Richard Gough, an editor of Camden's Britannia in which an illustration of the cross appeared, and a keen collector of antiquities, lived at nearby Gough Park from 1714 until his death in 1809; a situation known to Derek Mahoney. There is no mention of the cross in Richard Gough's papers, which he bequeathed to the Bodleian Library at Oxford. Nor is there any reference to the object in any catalogue of his collection, which was sold in 1810. Apart from this, it is impossible to believe that the cross could have found its way from Gough's collection to the bed of the lake at Forty Hall without some public reference to loss being made. Also, members of the Enfield Archaeological Society kept a close watch on the lake during the time it was being dredged. The operator of the machine used during these operations was known to the Society members concerned and he was quite sure that no lead cross had been found there.

In spite of his continued efforts, public interest in the cross waned and sadly Derek Mahoney, who by now was far from well and who had failed to resolve his legal problems, eventually took his own life. His cross was never found and the belief is that he destroyed it soon after showing it to the staff at the British Museum. He probably did this to avoid the possibility of the cross being discovered and the hoax exposed.

This story has now passed into local legend and like so many tales has gained in the telling. Only recently, during an exhibition by the Enfield Archaeological Society in the grounds of Forty Hall in 1995, members of the public were asking for more information about the discovery of a 'golden cross, a 'golden crown' and even a 'golden sword' (shades of Excalibur!) in the lake at Forty Hall.

Appendix Three — Arms Displayed on the Rainton Tomb

51 Arms displayed on the Rainton tomb

RAINTON: arms: Sable a chevron cotised between three cinquefoils or.
crest: A griffin's head coped sable beaked or charged on the neck with a cinquefoil of the last

MOULTON: arms: Gules a chevron argent fretty sable between three mullets pierced or.
crest: A griffin passant per pale gules and azure resting the dexter claw on a mullet or.

WOLSTENHOLME: arms: Lion passant guard between three pheons or (and hand sinister on shield)*
crest: An eagle displayed or standing on a snake mowed azure.
motto: '*In ardua virtus*' (Virtue in distress)

* the hand is shown in the drawing in ROBINSON but is not mentioned in the description of arms in CANSICK nor does it appear in BGA

References

ADVERTISER	*Enfield Advertiser* 17th December 1981
ALCOCK & HALL	N W Alcock & L Hall *Fixtures and Fittings in Dated Houses 1567-1763.* Council for British Archaeology 1994 p4
BAKER	Baker *History and Antiquities of Northamptonshire* Vol 1 1817 pp416-417
BEARD	Geoffrey Beard *Georgian Craftsmen and their Work* 1966 p63
BGA	*Burke's General Armory*
BRETON	Plan of Forty Hall Estate 1785
BUILDING NEWS	*The Building News* XXXV July 17th 1903 p67
BURIAL REG	*The Marriage, Baptismal and Birth Register 1571-1874*, Dutch Reformed Church, Austen Friars, London 1884 pp154 & 170
BURKE	*Burke's Commoners* 1838
CALENDAR (a)	Calendar of State Papers Domestic 1611-18 512; 1619-23 481
CALENDAR (b)	1683 263 339 349; 1683-4 4 48 282
CANSICK	Frederick Teague Cansick *A collection of curious and interesting epitaphs ... in the churchyards of Hornsey, Tottenham, Edmonton, Enfield, Friern Barnet and Hadley* 1875
CHANCERY	Chancery Proceedings 1758-1800 Bernau Index, Society of Genealogists for reference to the bundles and suit numbers in the Public Record Office
CLARK	Information from Miss P Clark, Deputy Registrar, The Royal Archives, Windsor Castle.
CLIFTON-TAYLOR	Alex Clifton-Taylor *The Pattern of English Building* 1972 p250
DAYES	Edward Dayes 1763-1804. The painting, a photograph of which was reproduced in *Country Life* (HARRIS) was supplied by Christie's of London but they can no longer find it nor have they any record of the present location of the painting. The photograph was subsequently displayed in WORSELY.
F H COLL	Collection of painting, prints and drawings at Forty Hall
FORD	Edward Ford and George Hodson *History of Enfield* 1873 p328
FSA	Minutes of the Society of Antiquaries 11th June 1789
GAPPER	C Gapper *Decorative Plasterwork in London 1540-c1640* MA Report University of London 1990 (Copy held in Forty Hall museum)
GAZETTE (a)	*Enfield Gazette and Observer* 27th August 1897
GAZETTE (b)	*ibid* 22nd October 1943
GENTS MAG (a)	*Gentleman's Magazine* 1790 Part II p90
GENTS MAG (b)	*ibid* 1785 Part II p1010
GENTS MAG (c)	*ibid* 1797 Part II p901
GENTS MAG (d)	*ibid* 1803 Part II p1157 and 1817 Part II p536
GENTS MAG (e)	Reproduced in Robinson II p239
GIBSON	*Short Account of Several Gardens Near London Upon a View of These in 1691.* From an original ms by J Gibson 16th January 1691. Summarised in *Archeaologia* Vol XII 1794 p189
GLRO	Greater London Record Office Middlesex Records Acc 16/1
GOUGH	Richard Gough and Others, Mss notes for a history of Enfield 1771-1809. In the Bodleian Library, Oxford
GUIDE	*Short Guide to Forty Hall* Information leaflet produced by London Borough of Enfield c1960 (Anon)
HARRIS	John Harris 'Classicism without Jones' *Country Life* CLXXIV No 40 October 4th 1990 pp152-155
HARWOOD	Elaine Harwood *Forty Hall An Architectural History.* Information leaflet, London Borough of Enfield 1990
HERBARIUM	Information from D F Chamberlain, Herbarium curator, Royal Botanical Gardens, Edinburgh
HERITAGE	*Enfield's Architectural Heritage* Enfield Preservation Society 1989 p17
HUNSDON	'Excavations at Hunsdon House in Hertfordshire 1983-1987'. A lecture given to the Enfield Archaeological Society in December 1989 by Clive Partridge, *Society News* 116 March 1990. See also PALACES p34 & 42 for cess pits at Elsyng Palace
KEANE	William Keane *The Beauties of Middlesex* 1850
KOCH	Rev. Edward H A Koch MA *Forty Hill Church and Parish* 1935
LAWSON	William Lawson *A new Orchard and Garden and the Country Housewife's Garden* 1618
LYSONS (a)	Daniel Lysons *The Environs of London* 2nd Edition 1811 Vol II p185
LYSONS (b)	*ibid* p209
LYSONS (c)	*ibid* p196
MCGUIRE	Personal correspondence with Dr A McGuire who, with Prof A Gomme, is gathering material for a book on smaller country houses
MEYER	Family tree of the Meyer family
MOLAS	Museum of London Archaeology Service report Site Code F0794, Nov 1994
OBSERVER (a)	*Meyers Observer* 29th June 1894

OBSERVER (b)	*ibid* 27th August 1897
OS	Ordnance Survey 25 inch plans Middlesex II 1865, 1895, 1913, 1936
P1620	Pew rents St Andrews church from 1620 Document 1105, Enfield Local History Library
P1894	Photographs dated 1894 in the Local History Library.
PALACES (a)	Ian K Jones & Ivy Drayton *The Royal Palaces of Enfield* 1984, Enfield Archaeological Society Research Report No 4 p14
PALACES (b)	*ibid* p9
PAM (a)	David Pam *History of Enfield* Vol I 1990 pp146-8. He gives a detailed account of the civil disturbances following these enclosures, citing references Duchy of Lancaster DL 5, 38 347 & DL 9 14
PAM (b)	*ibid* p355
PEARL	V Pearl *London and the Outbreak of the Puritan Revolution* 1961 pp304-5
PEVSNER	Nicholas Pevsner *Buildings of Middlesex* 1951 p53
POLICY (a)	Document Room Guildhall Library ref 11936/9
POLICY (b)	*ibid* 11936/8
PRO (a)	Public Record Office c12 20/7 17 23rd January 1770: cited by PAM p154
PRO (b)	Breton Eliab 1786 Prob 11/1137
PRO (c)	Breton Elizabeth 1790 Prob 11/1189
PRO (d)	c33 504 443 12th June 1799
PRO (e)	PCC 1797 Armstrong Edward Middx Nov 672
PRO (f)	c33 504 443
PRO (g)	Duchy of Lancaster 43 7 8
PRO (h)	DL 43 7 1
PRO (i)	DL 43 7 5
R1656	An abstract of all lands and tenements appertaining to the estate of Nicholas Rainton, Esq 1656 County Record Office 16/8
RCHM	*Royal Commission on Historical Monuments An Inventory of the Historical Monuments in Middlesex* 1937 pp23-24 — especially the handwritten reports of the commissioners. National Monuments Record Office in London
REID	Richard Reid *The Georgian House and its Details* 1989 p85
ROBINSON (a)	William Robinson *History and Antiquities of Enfield* Vol I 1823 p287
ROBINSON (b)	*ibid* I p197
ROBINSON (c)	*ibid* I p238
ROBINSON (d)	*ibid* I p68
ROBINSON (e)	*ibid* II p30
ROBINSON (f)	*ibid* I p237
SP 1773	Sales Particulars Forty Hall Estate 25th August 1773
SP PLAN	Plan attached to Sales Particulars Forty Hall Estate 1773
SP 1786	Sales Particulars Forty Hall 1786
SP FEB 1787	Sales Particulars Forty Hall Feb 1787
SP 1799	Sales Particulars Forty Hall 1799
SCHEDULE	Information from his son who was visiting Forty Hall to arrange for a memorial seat to his father who had lived in one of six cottages in St Georges Road in the ownership of H F Bowles. Bowles Settled Estates Schedule of Enfield Properties March 1938
SMITH	I am grateful to Eric Smith for providing me with this information, later published in *Society News* 91 December 1988
SOC NEWS (a)	*Society News: Bulletin of the Enfield Archaeological Society* 128 March 1993
SOC NEWS (b)	*ibid* 83 December 1981 & 84 March 1982
SOC NEWS (c)	*ibid* 86 September 1982, 87 December 1892, 88 March 1983, 89 June 1983, 110 September 1988, 111 December 1988, 113 June 1989
STUART	David Stuart *The Kitchen Garden* 1984 p29
SYKES	John Sykes 'The Hunt for the Deer Park of Elsyng' *Society News* 33 June 1969
TAYLOR	*Some Account of the Taylor Family* (printed for private circulation) cited in *Forty Hall, Enfield, Middlesex, The Residence of Sir Henry Bowles Bart JP DL Investigation made at the British Museum Library as to its Origin and History* (printed for private circulation 1942)
TIMES (a)	*The Times* 21st October 1797 p3
TIMES (b)	*ibid* 3rd April 1983
VCH	*Victoria County History: Middlesex* Vol V 1976 p227
VESTRY	Unfortunately, the volume of Vestry Orders containing this entry has been lost, but details are given in GOUGH
W1616	Bargain and Sale Earl of Salisbury to N Rainton of the Manor of Worcestors 4th July 1616 Hatfield Deeds 102/25
WARE	Isaac Ware *A Complete Body of Architecture* 1756
WHITAKER	C W Whitaker *An Illustrated Historical Statistical and Topographical Account of ... Enfield* 1911 p137
WITTRICK	A R Wittrick *Report on Selected Farm Buildings at Forty Hall, Enfield* English Heritage July 1994 (Revised March 1996)
WORSLEY	Giles Worsley *Classical Architecture in Britain — The Heroic Age* 1995
WRIGHT	Information from I V Wright, Archivist H M Customs and Excise Library Services